WRITE IT RIGHT

WRITE IT RIGHT
The Guide to Self-Publishing Your Best Book

Gwen Richardson

SECOND EDITION

Cover design by Rosamond Grupp

ISBN: 978-0980025095
ISBN-10: 0980025095

10 9 8 7 6 5 4 3 2

Printed in the United States of America

To my husband, Willie,
who helps me be the best me I can be

TABLE OF CONTENTS

INTRODUCTION

The fact that you are reading this book is a clear indication of your desire to write one of your own. More than ever before, authors have the freedom and opportunity to publish books on their own, without acquiring an agent and signing a book deal with a major publisher. Whether you are an aspiring first-time author or have already published multiple titles and wish to expand your knowledge about self-publishing, this book will help you avoid commonly-made mistakes and eliminate some of the legwork and research you would otherwise need to do on your own.

Your potential book may be a work of fiction -- a novel based on imaginary people, places, or events -- or it could encompass the broad spectrum of non-fiction, which includes research-based writing ranging from biographies and memoirs, to faith-based journals, to motivational and self-help books. The type of book you are writing matters little in the broad scheme of things. What is important is that you understand why you are writing your book, what elements your book should include, and how to market and promote it to the book-buying public.

After reading *Write It Right: The Guide to Self-Publishing Your Best Book*, you should be well on your way to succeeding as a self-published author.

CHAPTER 1

TEN GREAT REASONS TO SELF-PUBLISH

Self-publishing your book(s) can be an extremely daunting task, but it can also be a gratifying experience. In some cases, it can also be lucrative and generate a sizeable secondary income. The truly fortunate self-published author is able to turn a passion for writing into a full-time career.

The following are ten great reasons to self-publish your book.

Reason #1: No need to wait for validation from agents and major publishers.

If you have developed a book concept and have completed your manuscript, waiting for a green light from an agent or publisher can be nerve-racking and disappointing. Aspiring authors often send their manuscript to dozens of publishers, and receive a similar number of rejection letters in response. The rejection letters tend to be standard form letters and are seldom personalized. Authors often wonder if these publishers even bothered to read their manuscript. And there are a few publishers that simply do not respond to authors' queries at all. In short, the entire process can be disheartening. Meanwhile, you have wasted precious time awaiting an agent's or publisher's approval, when you could have had a finished product in hand had you published the book yourself.

Your book might represent the industry's next literary treasure, but readers will never know because agents and publishers didn't believe it was "marketable." It has been my experience that industry professionals tend to only be confident about the types of books that have a track record of success in the industry and they rarely break new ground. In the words of Bettye Griffin, author of several works of women's fiction and contemporary romance, "The general rule of traditional publishers is imitation, imitation, and more imitation."

I also believe that publishers are not nearly as good at spotting the next new thing in literature as they are signing authors who follow a particular model within a specific genre. Many industry breakthroughs are the result of a self-published author who builds a market on his own and is then "discovered" by the major publishing houses. If you think your book has the potential to be a solid seller, do not hesitate to make your book project a reality. Hire an editor and a graphic artist to design your cover and get it out there. Once your book's popularity reaches the eyes and ears of the major publishers, they are likely to offer you a book deal. They are constantly on the lookout for authors who are gaining traction on their own because it makes their jobs much easier.

Many well-known, successful authors got their start as self-publishers, including publisher and erotica author Zane, and E. L. James, author of the *Fifty Shades of Grey* series. Once these authors proved there was a market for their works, publishing companies were tripping all over themselves offering them lucrative publishing contracts.

Zane's story is particularly intriguing. A perpetual *New York Times* best-selling author, Zane is also a publisher and television producer. She initially decided to self-publish because she wanted to retain the creative license for her works. "I actually was offered several publishing deals by major houses, but all of them wanted me to change my writing style," she said, during a panel discussion about the future of black publishing at the 2012 Harlem Book Fair. "I decided I was not going to do that."

Zane self-published her first three books, *Sex Chronicles*, *Addicted* and *Shame On It All*. In June 1999, she also started her own publishing company, Strebor Books, which afforded her the opportunity to publish not only her own books, but those written by other authors as well. But Zane didn't start out with a burning desire to write books.

"I started writing short stories over the Internet in 1997," she said at the Book Fair. For three years, she offered her work to anyone who was interested at no charge. "Then a rumor got started that I had an actual book out. People were going to bookstores looking for my book [which didn't exist]. That's when publishing companies started contacting me, offering me book deals."

She initially turned them down, but she spent time doing research on book publishing, marketing and distribution. She decided to gauge the viability of a potential book by conducting a marketing test on her website where she sold ten of her short stories for $10. "I spent hours at Kinko's, copying those stories, binding them and mailing them. That's when I realized I had a market for my book." By the time her first book was released, she already had tons of consumers waiting to read it.

In September 2003, Zane signed a distribution deal with Simon & Schuster, and two years later her company, Strebor, became a full-fledged imprint. Strebor now publishes books in the categories of non-fiction, fiction, memoir, biography, contemporary romance, science fiction, Christian fiction, paranormal and romance.

Zane currently has more than 90 authors under her publishing umbrella. Of course, every self-publisher is not going to match Zane's achievements. But her enormous success is evidence that self-published authors can turn their passion for writing into moneymaking endeavors.

Reason #2: You retain the rights to your material.

When you self-publish, you retain the rights to your material. Most print-on-demand and other self-publishing entities receive only the non-exclusive license to publish and distribute the work for you.

When you sign a contract with a major publisher, however, you relinquish the rights to publish your book for five to seven years, depending upon the terms of your contract. The book essentially becomes their property to do with as they choose. That includes the book's content and cover design.

This also means that you cannot publish the book yourself in whole or in part, nor reap the direct revenues from its sales. Authors usually also relinquish eBook rights. In other words, your book could potentially sell hundreds of thousands of copies and you will receive only about $1.20 (8 percent for the first 10,000 copies) for each sale of a fifteen-dollar trade size paperback. (This is known as the royalties of your book sales.)

A lot of authors are unaware that, when they sign a contract with a major publisher and receive their advance, it may be two years or more before they see any additional money. The author has to wait until sales surpass the threshold covered by the advance against royalties. The advance is the much-anticipated upfront fee authors receive when they sign a deal with a publisher. It is an advance against the royalties your publisher expects you to generate within the first year your book is on sale.

Advances are usually paid in increments, with one-third paid upon signing the contract, one-third upon submission of a satisfactory manuscript, and one-third upon publication. For example, if you receive an advance of $5,000 from the publisher for a trade paperback book, those are funds paid upfront for sales of about 4,167 copies that the publisher expects you to generate during the early months of your book's release. Until that threshold of sales is reached, you receive no additional funds from the publisher.

In addition, royalties are only paid twice per year, so be prepared for long stretches of time with no income from your book sales. Furthermore, even if you have earned your advances, you still never know how much money, if any, you will receive during any given pay period. That is because, as the author, you never know how many books you have sold, nor how much of a reserve against returns is retained by the publisher for that pay period.

A reserve against returns is the amount of money the publisher holds in case bookstores return copies of unsold books. If a retail bookstore orders fifty copies of your book and only sells forty, the remaining ten copies are returned to the publisher for credit, and the publisher charges the credit against your earned royalties. In order to avoid overpaying an author, publishers will withhold a percentage of the author's royalties against returns.[1]

In addition, royalties are paid only on the sales of new books. Under current copyright laws, authors earn zero royalties from the sales of used books, no matter how many times the used books are resold.[2]

At the end of the five- to seven-year period, the publishing rights usually revert back to the author. Some authors have used their rights to re-release their titles that were previously out of print. They then offer the new editions via a print-on-demand source, which keeps their titles in circulation beyond the normal life of a book. An example is historical romance author Beverly Jenkins, whose book _Indigo_ was originally published in 1996 by Avon Books. (Romance novels stay in print for a much shorter period of time than do works of general fiction, so the publishing rights revert back to the author more quickly.) In 2000, Jenkins re-released the book as a print-on-demand title and the book is still selling consistently.

The purchase of book club rights, movie rights, merchandising rights and foreign language translation rights are generally separate and not part of a standard publishing contract. However, in some contracts, the author relinquishes those rights as well. Typically, audio, electronic and book club rights are considered non-negotiable by publishers. Conversely, even first-time authors should be able to retain either film and television, or foreign translation rights, or both.[3]

If you sign a book deal with a publisher, _always_ have a publishing attorney and/or a literary agent represent you to make sure your rights are protected. More information about the process of signing a deal with a major publisher is included in Chapter 21.

Reason #3: Retain a much greater proportion of revenue from book sales.

If you are a self-publisher and you pay a print-on-demand company a per-copy price for each book you order, you retain all of the revenue beyond your per-copy price. This amount is going to be many times greater than the royalties you would receive from a major publisher.

For example, if you have a 200-page book and your copies cost you $3 when you order them from the publisher, a book with a retail price of $15 will give you a net profit of $12. Of course, you'll have to deduct your costs for editing, book cover design, shipping and supplies, but, assuming these costs are less than $1,000 in total, you'll only need to sell a total of 84 books at the retail price to break even.

This example refers to the copies that the author can order directly from the publisher for the purposes of reselling them. Most print-on-demand companies will sell the books on their site for the full retail price and give the author a percentage of those sales. But, in most cases, the author can order books from the publisher at a deep discount and sell them directly to consumers.

This example, however, does not include copies sold via the publisher's website because the author receives a much lower percentage of the retail price for those. For books sold on the publisher's website, the author may receive anywhere from 20 to 45 percent of the retail price, depending upon the guidelines that the publisher has set. This is still a much higher percentage than the royalties you would receive from a traditional publisher. And print-on-demand companies usually pay authors for the proceeds on their book sales on a monthly basis, rather than on a semi-annual basis, as is the practice with major publishers.

The costs of converting your book to eBook form are minimal. Most print-on-demand companies have online tools you can use for the conversion. You can also hire a free-lance expert to perform this task. Amazon.com pays about 70 percent to the author for all eBooks sold in Kindle format. If you are consistently marketing your book, the revenue could be substantial.

By comparison, as stated previously, royalties from book sales with a major publisher are about 8 percent for trade paperbacks and mass market paperbacks. Depending upon the suggested retail price for your book, this can amount to anywhere between $0.40 and $1.20 per copy. Most publishing agreements now provide that an author's royalties are reduced for certain "discounted" sales. The reduced royalties rate for deep-discount sales may be either one-half the stipulated royalties or a percentage of the publisher's net receipts.[4]

Of course, you are likely to sell many more paper copies through a major publisher because of their greatly expanded book distribution and publicity. But the odds of a first-time author getting a book deal are decreasing as we speak.

The popularity of eBooks may make the prospect of a book deal with a major publisher less attractive for self-publishers, as some self-published authors are making more money doing it themselves than they ever could under the umbrella of a large publishing house. Author Bella Andre has been published by Hachette, Random House and Simon & Schuster, but she left the traditional publishing world several years ago to go it alone. She told *Forbes* magazine that she made over $1 million in 2011 and *Time* magazine that she made $2.4 million in 2012 by selling her own eBooks.[5]

Stephanie Bond is another self-published author whose sales for her self-published book, *Stop the Wedding*, have done well. Bond has been published by HarperCollins, Macmillan, Random House and others.[6]

In 2012, self-published author Kerry Wilkinson became Amazon's top seller in the United Kingdom when his Jessica Daniel detective novels sold more than 250,000 copies on Kindle.[7]

For the first time ever, a self-published title *Wait for You* by Jennifer L. Armentrout, under the pen name J. Lynn, hit number one on the Digital Book World EBook Best-Seller list in March 2013.[8]

The experiences of Andre, Bond, Wilkinson and Lynn are atypical. But their kind of success will become more commonplace as authors increase their knowledge and experience about marketing their books and develop their own footprints in the book marketplace.

Reason #4: The subject matter for your book can cover an unusual or controversial topic.

The publishing world will print controversial books, but only on certain subjects. Whatever hesitance publishers might have had for sexual topics in the past, there presently does not appear to be much in the sexual arena that they will not print. Some of today's best-selling books are erotic in nature, with no-holds-barred descriptions and language. Even within works of mainstream fiction, graphic sexual scenes are par for the course.

Books that, a generation ago, would have been deemed so provocative that they would have been mailed in brown paper wrappers are now front and center in brick-and-mortar store displays. However, there are other topics that publishers deem to be too narrow, too controversial, too confusing, too limited – oh, so many too's!

Yet, entire new genres have been created because authors believed in their work and were willing to introduce it to the world. J.K. Rowling's success with the Harry Potter series is a case in point. The British author wrote her first book as a single mother on welfare. It was published under the name J.K. Rowling (her first name is Joanne) because her publisher thought that a woman's name would not appeal to the target audience of young boys. How wrong they were!

Rowling's books have sold to boys and girls, men and women, worldwide. They have generated more than $1 billion in book sales, and billions more in movie ticket sales and merchandising. Rowling's net worth in 2012 was estimated to be approximately $1 billion and the Harry Potter brand is estimated to be worth more than $15 billion.[9]

Sometimes a publishing house will accept your manuscript, but then the editors will slice large swaths out of your narrative in order to make it more "mainstream." In some cases, they might alter your narrative entirely. To be sure, every book needs to be edited, and text will sometimes need to be removed or reworded to improve the quality of the end product. But some publishing houses will make suggestions based on their own biases or narrow viewpoint.

For example, authors have told me that publishers will request that they include more graphic sexual scenes in their books to make them more appealing; or that the author change the language to make the characters sound more "ethnic" or "black." African-American authors are generally expected to have a nearly all-black cast of characters in their books. Breaking out of this stereotype can be extremely difficult when dealing with traditional publishers.

Such was the case with author Millenia Black, who self-published *The Great Pretender* in 2006. Black's novel explored universal themes like infidelity, betrayal, and internal conflict over one's misdeeds. The novel included mostly white characters and its cover was race-neutral.[10]

Sales for *The Great Pretender* were brisk and Black was offered a book deal by Penguin. The company initially didn't realize that Black was African-American but, when company representatives found out, they used brown-skinned models for the new *Great Pretender* cover. This decision was made despite the fact that the characters were not African-American. When Penguin attempted to market the book to a more limited, black audience, the author protested.[11]

Black argued that being categorized as an African-American author would limit her sales potential, as her book would be shelved in the African-American literature section, rather than among general fiction titles. Penguin ignored her wishes, so she sued. The parties settled in 2008 and Black cannot discuss the details of the case. But here is how she described her experience to a book industry blogger:

"I always dreamed of being like Jackie Collins or Danielle Steel. Of having a career that had nothing to do with my color, everything to do with my stories. I thought there was equal opportunity."

But Black maintains confidence that her stories will "find their way into the American mainstream, where they belong."[12]

As a self-publisher, there is no need to stifle your creativity. Step outside of the rigid boxes major publishers create. If you have the ability to develop a winning synopsis that will entice people to purchase your book in a bookstore or click the "buy it" button online, as well as the ability to generate word-of-mouth buzz, that's what will determine your success.

If you think your subject matter is worthy of a book, then you can publish it without regard for the whims, fetishes and proclivities of the major publishers. Don't worry. If your book sales take off, they'll come 'a callin'.

Reason #5: There is no pressure to produce a book (or in some cases, two books) every year.

When authors sign with traditional publishers, they agree to produce at least one book every year for the length of the contract. There are some exceptions, but this is the general rule for fiction writers. This is problematic. An author's first book may be fantastic. After all, some first books take five to ten years to write, or longer, and during that time, the author has had the opportunity to massage every phrase and ponder each plot twist.

However, the author's second book and subsequent books are often rushed, and the haste is obvious to the reader. One of the worst experiences in the world for a reader is to read an author's first book and be nearly awestruck, only to be completely let down by the second effort. The reader is left wondering, "What happened?"

Over the years I have had many conversations with authors who are under pressure to complete a book by a deadline. The deadline is two weeks away, and they are only halfway through the required word count. They will sometimes go into seclusion in order to maintain their focus, but it is still challenging to conjure up a compelling storyline in short order.

Writing is not something that can be forced; it requires some sort of inspiration. Some gifted writers are able to churn out books in rapid fashion, but, for others, it takes much more time for the ideas to percolate.

As a self-published author, you are under no such pressure. You can write one book every three years or three books in one year. You are able to do what works for you.

Reason #6: Today, it's so inexpensive.

A decade ago, the cost of publishing was out of reach for most aspiring authors. Traditional printing presses required runs of at least 5,000 copies for the printing job to be cost-effective. The cost to the author could easily be $5,000 or more.

Authors would then have thousands of books to sell. They would discover how difficult it is for an individual author to move 5,000 copies of a book. Most of these authors ended up with boxes of books in their garages that gathered dust and were eventually discarded.

In the brave new world of self-publishing, print-on-demand and eBooks, an author's upfront costs are minimal. Once the manuscript is completed and edited, it can be uploaded and put into eBook form at virtually no cost. Editing fees can vary, depending on the page count. A professional-looking book cover is still required for an eBook, but the author can get both the editing and the book cover done for under $1,000 using online freelance sources.

Rather than print hundreds or thousands of copies of books that sit in boxes waiting to be sold, the author can print a few copies at a time at a minimal cost per copy and sell them at his or her own pace. Once those copies are sold, the funds can be reinvested into printing more so that the book-printing expense is always manageable.

Reason #7: A relatively small amount of sales can still lead to success.

In general, publishers require sales above 10,000 copies in a relatively short time frame to recoup their overhead costs for publishing your book. These costs can be substantial (e.g., editors, graphic designers, marketers, publicists, etc.). That is one of the reasons why major publishers invest so heavily in ensuring early sales results.

The first week of a new book's release is monitored carefully, similar to the box office results at a movie theater. The first three months of sales data are crucial. According to data collected from major publishers, for most books, 80 to 90 percent of sales occur in the first six months of publication, barring a major development, like a movie deal, major media coverage, or instant celebrity status.[13]

Publishers make a significant financial investment in their authors, even though these costs can be appropriated among dozens or even hundreds of authors. Because of economies of scale (increase in efficiency of production as the number of goods being produced increases), the publishers' overhead costs to support each individual author decrease as they add more and more authors to their roster.

As a self-publisher, you don't have all of the fixed overhead costs. Plus, you can allocate your additional expenditures at your own pace and according to your own budget.

You don't need to sell tons of books every month to earn extra income from your writing. An additional $1,000 to $2,000 monthly net profit from book sales may be attractive enough to pursue the effort and meet your long-term career goals.

Reason #8: Your book can be released more quickly.

When a publisher accepts your manuscript and pays you an advance against royalties, the average amount of time it takes for your book to actually hit bookstore shelves is one full year. It may even take longer if the publisher requires major rewrites or edits; or if they have a similar book being released during the same time frame by one of their "A list" authors and delay your book's release date to avoid marketing conflicts. Meanwhile, you're sitting on pins and needles, waiting for the day when you will finally have your published book in your hands and it will be available for readers to purchase.

This delay can sometimes mean that you miss opportunities for speaking engagements, or media interviews, or even to release the initial book's sequel. Sometimes the subject your book addresses can be a "hot topic" at the time, but, a year later, some of that heat may have dissipated. Interested parties may have moved on to something else.

When you self-publish, you can release your book as soon as the manuscript is complete and the editing has been done. You can strike while the iron is hot and while your audience's interest is at its apex. Your book does not have to be in limbo, awaiting a future date when the publisher will give a green light to release it.

Reason #9: You can publish across multiple genres.

Publishers tend to prefer the cookie-cutter approach to book categorization. They like to place authors within a narrow box and have them perform the same sorts of tasks over and over again.

If a writer's first few books with a publisher are romance titles, for example, the publisher will want the author to stay within that genre. They believe that the author has already built an audience in that genre and will want him or her to continue selling to that audience with future book releases. In fact, sometimes the publisher will insist on it and, contractually, prevent the author from submitting any other books that do not fit within that genre.

But suppose you think you would do well writing a book on a related topic, such as relationships, which is a non-fiction category? It is highly unlikely that you will get encouragement and support from your publisher. In their minds, you're locked in to whatever category they have selected for you. Breaking out of such a rigid box may be extremely difficult. Some authors will actually sign a contract with a different publisher (if their existing contract will allow it) in order to write books that fall under other categories.

As a self-publisher, you are not bound by any of these restrictions. If you want to deviate from your normal writing style and try your hand at something different, you have the flexibility to do so. Of course, you may have already established a name and a market for your previous work, but that doesn't mean you cannot sell a different book to those same customers, or acquire new customers in a new genre. In other words, you can expand your reach and access an entirely new set of readers by writing across multiple genres.

I have experienced this personally as a self-published author. My first book, published in 2008, was non-fiction and sold relatively well. But I had always wanted to try my hand at writing fiction. I wrote a mystery that also sold relatively well.

Since then I have self-published a total of eight titles—all but one of which are non-fiction--and plan to continue writing. I would like to continue to expand the types of readers I reach, thereby, broadening my readership overall.

When I go out to events and speak to an audience, I usually sell at least four of my books, depending on the audience. Some buyers will purchase all of them; some will purchase only one, depending on their interest.

Reason #10: Book deals are nothing like they used to be.

Several years ago it seemed that almost every author was getting a six-figure book deal. Folks were self-publishing books, selling a couple thousand copies and were then offered incredibly attractive contracts. A select few authors who experienced publishing success were offered their own imprints and were assigned a cadre of authors under their publishing umbrellas. People assumed that world would last forever. It didn't.

Publishers discovered that they had overestimated future sales of some authors who received lucrative book deals. Once the publishing houses had gotten burned by expensive contracts with authors whose book sales had fizzled, they began to over-compensate in the opposite direction. Here is how the book industry is currently structured.

There is a small group of "A list" authors who still get lucrative book contracts and advances. These are either celebrities or people who have a well-established track record of book sales.

Since there is only so much money to go around, the remaining authors get next to nothing. These days, the average debut fiction author with an agent and a publishing contract gets an advance of less than $5,000. This advance is not paid in a lump sum. It is paid out in three or four installments over a one- to two-year period from the time the deal is closed.

And multi-book deals are becoming less and less common, even for established authors. If your pipe dream is to collect at least a five-figure check when your manuscript is accepted, you might need to pinch yourself and wake up. Those days are gone.

Even for those authors who are lucky enough to get book deals, they receive much less support from their publisher than before. Authors are expected to do their own marketing and promotion. Book tours paid for by the publisher are limited to the "A list" authors. And don't forget that the agent, if you have one, receives 15 percent of every dollar that your book generates, including of the paltry advance you will be paid.

Another understandable industry development is that publishers have become more insistent that authors who receive hefty advances actually produce their books. Penguin Books, for example, recently filed lawsuits against several prominent writers who failed to deliver books for which they received sizeable contractual advances.[14]

- **Elizabeth Wurtzel**, author of *Prozac Nation*, signed a $100,000 deal in 2003 to write a book for teenagers to help them cope with depression. Penguin wants Wurtzel to return her $33,000 advance.
- Blogger **Ana Marie Cox** signed a $325,000 deal in 2006 to author a humorous examination of the next generation of political activists. Penguin wants its $81,250 advance returned.
- Holocaust survivor **Herman Rosenblat** is being asked to repay a $30,000 advance he received in 2008. He was expected to produce a

book about how he met his wife of 50 years in a Nazi concentration camp.[15]

- Well-known record producer, rapper, and clothing designer **Sean "P. Diddy" Combs** was sued in 2005 by Random House for recovery of a $300,000 advance for an allegedly undelivered memoir due in 1999.[16]

In addition, publishers have the right to demand the return of a portion of the advance an author received, if his or her book sales do not amount to enough to earn the royalties that were originally advanced. Although this rarely happens in practice, it is possible, depending upon the terms of the contract.

If you still remain committed to acquiring a book deal with a traditional publisher, more information about what to expect is included in Chapter 21.

CHAPTER 2

TEN MAJOR CHALLENGES SELF-PUBLISHED AUTHORS FACE

The previous chapter detailed the positive aspects of being a self-published author. But there are, indeed, challenges to going it alone. These challenges may appear to be daunting, but are not insurmountable. Following are ten of the primary obstacles that authors confront when they self-publish.

Challenge #1: Self-publishing can be overwhelming.

When an author signs with a traditional publisher, the publisher invests a tremendous amount of resources in publishing his or her book. Expenditures include, but are not limited to:

- Editors, either on staff or contracted, to take the book through several editing phases
- Typesetting and proofreading
- Marketers, to develop pre-sale and post-release promotion strategies
- Graphic designers to create presentations and design covers
- Printing and mailing costs, for catalogs and brochures that are sent to book buyers
- Point-of-sale market research

- Book printing costs
- Shipping, warehousing and distribution costs
- Endorsements
- Advance review copies to key professionals in the book trade

The collective expenditures form a tremendous infrastructure which kicks into high gear whenever an author's book is scheduled for release. In addition, these resources help generate sales and publicity and are borne entirely by the publisher.

Most first-time authors do not realize what they are getting into. Most believe that once they write the book and get it printed, their work is done. The self-published author has to bear these expenses and handle these tasks alone or exclude them altogether. Also, the author must either possess some of the skills and talents required to perform these tasks, or pay someone to perform them. The entire process can be so costly and overwhelming that most self-published authors exhaust their resources and give up after only a few months. Staying motivated and continuing your work once your book is published will require discipline and dedication.

Challenge #2: Your book(s) will have limited distribution.

An author receives a tremendous amount of satisfaction from the experience of going into a bookstore and seeing his or her book on the shelves for readers to thumb through and, ultimately, purchase. If you are signed with a major publisher, the company should already be well established with distributors and book retailers to make this a reality.

As a self-published author, the likelihood of the paper version of your book being available in bookstores nationwide is slim to none. Because of the substandard production quality of the majority of self-published books, bookstores are wary about stocking them in their stores.

You may have some success with getting independent bookstores in your local area to carry your book. Some will do so on a consignment basis, which means that you provide them with a limited supply of books that they can put on the shelves to see if their customers will purchase copies. The stores only pay you if they actually sell your books. The stores receive a standard 40 percent of the retail price for carrying your book and you, as the author, receive 60 percent. Some stores may require that they receive a higher percentage, but 40 percent is the standard for the book industry.

But there are some drawbacks to consignment arrangements with bookstores. First, unless the books are placed in a prominent place, they will likely be overlooked by customers. Second, if you have books in several stores in your area, you will need to track outstanding inventory for each store. Even if you have some sales, the cost of travel expenses (e.g., gas and time) that it takes to collect your sales revenue will likely be greater than the income your sales will produce. Finally, and unfortunately, some bookstores will sell your books, refuse to return them, and keep all of the revenue. Your options for forcing them to do the right thing will be limited since the sums are not large enough to pursue litigation in small claims court. Here's a word to the wise: Be cautious about consignment arrangements.

All bookstores respond to demand and if your book has demonstrated demand, bookstores will acquire copies by purchasing them from you or your publisher at the wholesale price and display them on their shelves. After all, a bookstore only makes money if a sale is made and all stores want to have items that the public wants to buy. More detailed information about approaching bookstores to persuade them to carry your book is included in Chapter 20.

Challenge #3: Some consumers may not take you seriously.

Unfortunately, some consumers do not take self-published authors seriously in terms of their craft and the book they produce. As mentioned in challenge #2 above, with the proliferation of self-published books in the marketplace, overall their reputation is less than stellar. The relative ease with which new authors can get their books published has also led to a large quantity of books that probably should not have been published or, at the very least, needed some professional massaging before they were released to the public.

In addition, many consumers believe that if your writing is of high quality, you would have already obtained a contract with one of the big New York-based publishing houses. For some consumers, unless your book has the look and feel of one produced by one of the major publishers, such as Simon & Schuster, Penguin or Random House, they perceive it to be an inferior product.

One way to counter this perception is by producing a book that, on first glance, looks like one that is professionally prepared. In this regard, a slick-looking cover and a book that is thoroughly edited become essential.

Challenge #4: Most bookstores won't carry your book.

This challenge was introduced in challenge #2 regarding limited distribution. Most bookstores shy away from accepting self-published books for a number of reasons:

- The book's presentation does not meet industry standards in terms of cover design, layout and editing;
- The books are usually not returnable, and retailers expect to be able to return books to the publisher if their sales are lackluster;
- Carrying these books wreaks havoc with bookstore accounting, as dealing with dozens

of individual authors is a lot more cumbersome from a bookkeeping standpoint; and

- Unfortunately, self-published books have garnered a less-than-stellar reputation and some bookstores refuse to accept any books that are self-published.

Again, you may have limited success with bookstores in your local community, but do not be surprised if a telephone canvass of bookstores produces little to no results. You may still be able to host a book signing or launch party at one of your local bookstores. More details on how to succeed with bookstores is included in Chapter 20.

Challenge #5: It will probably take you much longer to build a reading audience.

Authors who are successful develop a base of readers, known as a "reading audience," who will read almost any book they write. This audience is built after years of successful book sales, but nearly guarantees a certain level of book sales and revenue anytime the author releases a new book.

As a self-published author, it will take you much longer to build your reading audience. You will start with a few dozen readers – mostly friends and family -- and then expand your base over time. Increasing your base of readers will require a consistent marketing effort and the topic of marketing will be covered in Chapters 17, 18 and 19.

Challenge #6: You will not receive an advance and will need to use your own financial resources.

Even though advances paid by major publishers have decreased over the years, these funds are a lump sum payment an author can use to compensate him or her for the time expended writing the book. As a self-publisher, you do not receive any funds upfront from another entity and you will have to use your own resources to publish and market your book. The amount expended may be substantial and there is no guarantee that your book venture will be profitable.

You are taking a risk but, on a positive note, you are betting on yourself. If you are willing to work hard, work smart and be diligent, you can generate substantial revenue from your book venture.

Challenge #7: It is considered to be more prestigious to be signed with a major publisher.

When an author can hold his or her head high and proclaim, "I just signed a book deal with Simon & Schuster [or substitute any of the other major New York-based publishers]," the author has a sense of pride and major accomplishment. Authors know that, as one among the elite group of writers with book contracts, they already have the stamp of approval from entities within the book industry. They will be able to walk into a bookstore chain or independent bookstore and see a visible display their books on the store's shelves.

They have the opportunity for their books to be on the most respected best-sellers' lists and to receive national recognition. (It is nearly impossible for a self-published book to be listed on the *New York Times* best-sellers list.) Although self-published authors will occasionally experience national breakthroughs, these occur in rare instances.

Challenge #8: Self-published authors can often feel isolated and disconnected.

Being a self-published author can often be a lonely sojourn. You spend months or years in solitude as you write your masterpiece. Then, once you finally get it published, you arrange a book launch, contact bookstores and libraries, make calls to media outlets, reach out to book clubs – and these tasks are usually done by you or with the help of a family member or friend. Some weeks you will have some successes, but many times you will experience rejection, loss and a sense of failure.

That is why it is so important to connect with other authors and people in the book industry. Make it a habit to review your local newspaper's listings and book-related social media platforms for book events in your area. For most of them, admission will be free. You'll be able to learn from the experiences of other authors, as well as interact with readers and bookstore owners.

During these events, you may get an opportunity to have a direct conversation with the manager or event planner. Perhaps you can inquire about the guidelines or policies for hosting book events or getting your books included in the store's inventory. In most cases, if you support a store's events, the manager will be more open to at least hearing about your book and considering it for its audience.

Challenge #9: Most book clubs will refuse to select your book as a featured book among their readers.

Like bookstores, book clubs have become selective about the books their members choose to read. Book clubs are usually locally-based groups that meet monthly to discuss a book selected by their members. These groups are comprised of avid readers who are veterans when it comes to consuming and evaluating literature. Because the members are spending their own personal funds, they tend to be selective about investing in books that are not produced in a professional fashion.

Some book clubs refuse to even consider self-published books because they have been "burned" in the past with poorly edited and published material. However, there are ways to maneuver around this obstacle, and some of these methods will be presented in Chapter 18.

Challenge #10: You probably will not generate as much money as you would through a major publisher.

In light of the nationwide distribution and marketing advantages that a major publisher will have when compared to the personal contacts you may have at your disposal, you are unlikely to generate a comparable amount of revenue as a self-published author. However, there are exceptions and a number of self-published authors generate six-figure incomes through their book sales.

Most of the authors who generate high incomes have multiple published books, so it would be unwise to expect to generate a six-figure income following the release of your first book. But, as you continue to write and publish, the cumulative effect of the revenue generated by multiple titles will be tangible. The more books you produce, the more you will sell.

CHAPTER 3

WHY ARE YOU WRITING YOUR BOOK?

Before you begin the writing process, it is a good idea to spend some time reflecting. Understanding the reason(s) why you are writing your book will go a long way towards determining its contents and the sequence of the narrative or information presented.

There are a myriad of reasons why people become first-time authors. Some of the most common reasons are as follows:

- To share life experiences that they would like to record for the sake of posterity. As individuals approach their retirement years, they will often have years of family or individual experiences that they would like to chronicle. The information, which may include photos, family recipes, letters, official documents, and other materials, may span generations, and the author may believe the most effective way to share it all is by writing a book.
- To undergo a therapeutic exercise following the loss of a child, spouse or other close loved one. Putting the details of those experiences on

paper can be cathartic and can help ease the writer's emotional pain.

- To share solutions to life's challenges with others. For every individual who has overcome a challenging experience, there are hundreds (perhaps thousands) of others who have had similar experiences. These successes can include bouncing back after bankruptcy, recuperating after a major illness, recovering from alcoholism, or obtaining a college degree. Writing a book to assist others on the road to recovery or success can provide readers with information they otherwise would not have.

- To provide "how to" assistance on topics that mystify large segments of the population. Rather than reinvent the wheel, consumers are often looking for books that will help them solve a specific problem or expand their knowledge of a particular area or field of study. Whether the subject is repairing cars, computers, or writing a book, an author can achieve success by transferring her knowledge to others in book form.

- To amass information or data in one, easily-referenced source. Reference books that aggregate volumes of information and compile them in one handy tool can often be winners in the book marketplace. These books save consumers, educators and others time, money, and frustration.

- To exact revenge on relatives, former friends or business associates who have harmed them, physically, financially or emotionally. Family turmoil and drama can leave emotional scars and some may suffer in silence for years. Writing a tell-all book is a way to air dirty laundry, get things out in the open and let the world know what actually happened from the author's point of view.

- To further their careers or to enhance their businesses. For professionals who embark upon speaking careers, publishing at least one book is almost essential. A published book enhances the author's credibility and also provides an additional revenue stream, especially for individuals who already have a popular blog, radio show or seminar series. It also establishes the professional as an expert in his or her field.

- To share information about historical facts or individuals that could be of interest to others. Where would our world be without biographies and historical books that make the public aware of people and events that hold significance for our past, present and future? Authors conduct much-needed research, interview relevant individuals, visit historic sites, and document and organize it all into historical books.

- To share an interesting storyline. Talented fiction writers find genuine pleasure using their creativity to develop a plot and storyline that others can enjoy. One storyline or interesting main character can easily become a series of tales that span decades of publishing success.

- To share the product of an active imagination. Some writers have imaginations that are absolutely amazing. They can conjure up new planets, new worlds, new tribes, or new creatures, and their words can create a lens into an imaginary future or the distant past. If an author presents these visions in a coherent, readable and engaging fashion, his or her books could become the next Lord of the Rings book series.
- To get rich by selling a million copies of their first book, even though they have not built a readership base and are completely unknown in the publishing world and in the media. This is the pipe dream of a lot of aspiring authors. The odds of this happening are slim to none. If you're writing a book as a get-rich-quick scheme, don't bother.

Write It Right is designed to primarily benefit aspiring authors who want to write their books for commercial purposes, to sell to readers in a niche market or within the general market. But those who desire to write books for the purpose of a family project or heirloom can also benefit from the information included in the following chapters.

CHAPTER 4

UNDERSTANDING THE STATE OF THE BOOK MARKET

The book market is constantly evolving. Only a few years ago, all books were read in paper form and customers could only buy a book by walking into a brick-and-mortar store, purchasing it from a street vendor's table, checking it out from a library, or ordering it online and waiting for it to arrive in the mail. Now books in digital form -- eBooks -- are an integral, and rapidly growing, segment of the book market.

Author Earnings, a company established by authors and for authors that gathers data on book sales—both print and digital, estimates that 485,538,000 eBooks were sold in 2016.[17] That is nearly half a *billion* eBooks! It is expected that the percentage of eBook sales will only continue to grow in the coming years. This means that if you're planning to write a book, both the eBook and paper formats are essential.

However, the growth of the eBook market may have plateaued. According to the Association of American Publishers, eBook sales declined 18.7 percent over the first nine months of 2016, while paperback sales were up 7.5 percent over the same period, and hardback sales increased 4.1 percent.[18]

However, because the Association limits its surveys to 1,200 publishers and largely ignores the vastly expanding market of authors who are publishing independent, the may not accurately reflect the entire book market.

With the constant evolution of the book market in mind, the paper version of your book is still important because most books are still read in paper form. The tactile experience of reading books on paper increases the reader's retention of the information, and it is also easier on the eyes.[19] For face-to-face encounters, such as speaking engagements and book expos, the attendees expect to be able to purchase an autographed copy of the author's book. Also, for millions of readers, a book is not an actual product unless it is tangible and in paper form, either in hardcover or paperback.

For the paper version of your book, with print-on-demand as a viable option, you no longer need to print thousands of copies of your book and store the boxes in your garage as inventory for future sales opportunities. You can have your cover professionally designed, print small quantities and reorder as needed, reserving valuable resources for your marketing and promotion efforts.

Creating the eBook version of your book is equally important. The eBook provides you with the ability to get your book to the marketplace quickly and at a low cost. You will still need to have the cover of your book professionally designed; in fact, this is even more important for the digital version, since the cover is all the potential purchaser of your book will see before making the buying decision. The importance of your book cover is explained in more detail in Chapter 10.

Here are some interesting statistics on the book publishing industry in the U.S. These stats may either intimidate you or inspire you, depending on your point of view.

- According to the Association of American Publishers, close to $30 billion is spent annually on books in the U.S.[20]
- Despite the rapid growth of eBooks, brick-and-mortar retail remains the number one sales distribution channel for publishers.[21]
- The average U.S. nonfiction book is now selling fewer than 250 copies per year and fewer than 3,000 copies over its lifetime.
- The average self-published book sells a total of 150 to 200 copies, and that's mostly to friends and family.[22]
- Self-published eBooks sell for an average price of $2.76.[23]
- Romance is the largest category in Ebook sales.[24]
- Surveys consistently find that women read more books than men, especially when it comes to fiction. The Associated Press (AP) found that, among avid readers, the typical woman reads nine books in a year, while the typical man reads only five. Women read more than men in all categories except for history and

biography. Finally, men account for only 20 percent of the fiction market.[25]

- Ninety-six percent of urban fiction online sales are eBooks.[26]

- Amazon.com has more than 20 million books listed for sale on its site. Some of these titles are out of print and are being sold by third-party sellers, but that is still a huge number of titles available for sale in the book marketplace.

- The most important factor in selling books is *marketing*. An exemplary case is the *50 Shades of Grey* trilogy. Publicity sells books; even poorly written books can sell millions of copies (but usually only when the book is published by one of the large publishing firms that has distribution through all book retailers). For first-time authors or those who have not yet built an audience, the books must be well-written, well-edited and well-promoted.

The good news is that, even with increased competition, a book that sells 10,000 copies will generate substantial income for the author – how much exactly depends on the retail price, the percentage the author earns, and the associated expenses the author incurs. For example, if you make a net profit of $7 per paperback book, selling 10,000 copies gives you a total profit of $70,000. Not bad for doing something you actually enjoy!

For an eBook that sells at a retail price of $4.99, the author receives about 70 percent of the retail price, or $3.49. That amount is nearly all profit since there are no printing, mailing or storage costs for eBooks. The eBook format also allows an author to quickly distribute internationally and capture readers worldwide.

The eBook market has been growing rapidly for the past several years, but there are signs that books on paper will be around for years to come. According to a recent article on the Salon.com website, 75 percent of readers still prefer their books in paper form.[27] Therefore, authors should still be prepared to publish most of their titles in both formats.

Be Realistic

As an aspiring author, you must be realistic. *Just because you publish a book, people are not automatically going to buy it.* Don't expect your book sales to take off like a rocket. Months and months of consistent marketing and promotion will be required to realize even a modest amount of sales.

Also, don't expect that publishing your first book will put you on the map as an accomplished author. A more typical scenario is that an author publishes at least five books and it is one of the later ones that finally expands his or her reach. At that point, sales of the earlier titles may also increase as readers of the later book want to explore the author's previous work.

If you are really serious about writing, publishing five books over a period of five to ten years is an achievable goal. Understanding the landscape of the book market will allow you to develop realistic benchmarks and remain motivated.

CHAPTER 5

DETERMINING YOUR BOOK'S SUBJECT MATTER

What should I write about? This is the question that authors often ask themselves when they contemplate launching their book projects. The answer I hear most often goes something like this: "I want to write a book about my life because I've had some very interesting and dramatic experiences. It would be an international best seller."

This is a common response because most first books are autobiographical. Even works of fiction often contain some autobiographical elements. Most people think their personal life story is fodder for a best-selling book and one of the first tenets of writing a book is indeed to write about something you know. Yet, biographies are generally not widely read or commercially successful, except in the following instances:

1. A celebrity or famous person writes a tell-all book, or a biography is written by a third-party about a famous individual, living or deceased.
2. An author's life story is shaped so it has relevance to others in similar situations *and* the

book receives an above-average amount of national publicity.

Why? Because no one really wants to know about someone's life story unless that person is *already famous.*

That's why it's so important to write your book with the above caveat of shaping your narrative to also apply to the reader. As a person who is virtually unknown in the book market, you'll need to broaden your potential audience as widely as possible to be successful. Remember: People read books to be either entertained or informed. With that in mind, you can craft your life story so that it informs others and provides some practical tips the reader can actually use. Or you can craft your life story to make it entertaining or provocative by developing your book as a work of fiction.

Here is an example of how you can make your life story relevant. I recently spoke with a member of my church who told me that she took care of both of her aging parents, who suffered from Alzheimer's. She thought her experience could be helpful to others and would be an excellent concept for a book. One thing she should *not* do is give the book a title like, *Jane Doe: My Story.* This says nothing about the content of the book and would be of interest only to people within her direct sphere of influence (e.g., friends, family, acquaintances and business associates).

An example of a more marketable title would be: *How to Care for Aging Parents with Alzheimers*

Without Losing Your Mind. The audience the first title appeals to is small and includes primarily the author's family and friends. The second title greatly increases the book's appeal and makes it relevant to individuals around the world who are experiencing similar challenges.

As mentioned above, another viable option is that a personal story can be converted into a work of fiction. In this instance, the names, places, dates and circumstances should be altered to avoid legal repercussions and angry relatives. Authors often write accounts of famous people as fiction in order to be able to alter some of the actual events or characters, making them more interesting, dramatic or complete.

There are many viable options for book topics, but you should write about a subject that interests you and about which you are passionate. A high level of interest on your part will make the writing process shorter and more pleasurable. Your enthusiasm will be reflected in your writing style and tone. You will be motivated to write consistently and your words will flow more freely.

If your topic is related to your profession, the writing process will greatly expand your professional knowledge and potentially, over the course of research, bolster your network of experts in your field. You will want to contact some of these individuals, interview them, and include their expertise within your book in appropriate chapters or sections.

If you have a concept for a novel, develop a plot and characters that will make your book stand out in the marketplace. Don't write the same stories you have been reading; write something fresh, new and different. You may want to test out your plot ideas within a small circle of friends who are themselves avid readers to see if the ideas are viable. You don't have to reveal your entire story, and you probably shouldn't, but create a 30-second pitch (essentially a synopsis) to see how they respond. More information about developing the plot of your book is provided in Chapter 9.

Whatever process you utilize to decide on your book's topic, try to avoid months of vacillation. Some aspiring authors remain in the "aspiring" mode for years because they are indecisive. They change book themes, concepts and storylines multiple times until they are not sure where to even begin. Don't let this be you.

CHAPTER 6

IDENTIFYING YOUR POTENTIAL TARGET AUDIENCE

Your book is more than simply a work of literature; it is a product. In the same way that a diet beverage or laundry detergent is a product that must address the needs of the end user, your book must address the needs of a particular segment of the reading population that wants to be either entertained or informed. Before you start the writing process, you'll need to determine the intended end user of your product. In other words, who is your target audience and which readers are most likely to read your book?

Is your intended audience primarily your relatives and close friends? If so, your book project may not be a commercial product. It may have a limited appeal that can be established instead as a family project or heirloom. This is perfectly all right if that is your goal.

A commercial product has the potential to sell at least 1,000 copies. A thousand copies may not seem like a lot of books, but remember that most self-published books experience sales of between 150 to 200 copies, on average. If you are planning to write a book to sell commercially, identifying and understanding your target audience will go a long way toward increasing your sales and odds of success.

During my book writing seminars and consultations with aspiring and established authors, one of the questions I often pose to aspiring authors is: What is the target audience for your book? or, Who is most likely to read your book? If their answer is "everybody," then I know they really don't understand the book market and the nuances of market segmentation. They simply have not thought through the concept of marketing their book. This is a common issue that, frankly, applies to most first-time authors, most of whom seem to believe that simply because they wrote a book, thousands of people will hear about it and want to buy it.

The market of book readers is highly segmented with multiple niches. There are dozens of book genres and, within each genre, there is further stratification. For example, children's books represent a large segment of the market. Yet there are books for toddlers, books for children who are just starting to read (ages 4 to 6), others targeting elementary-age children, others for middle-schoolers, and still others for the teen market.

Fiction is a huge category with multiple subgenres, such as romance, mystery, suspense, historical, urban, Christian, classics, supernatural, crime, and fantasy. Although some people read books across multiple genres, most tend to read within a few similar genres. Everyone has some categories of books they will reject entirely; some may decline individual books within their preferred genres because of other factors, such as a high page count or a synopsis that failed to inspire them.

There are other factors that affect a reader's book-buying decision. For example, through an author's or publisher's marketing and promotion efforts, readers may become aware of a book on a topic that interests them, so they make a purchase that is outside their norm. A reader's friend may describe a book she read recently with such passion and fervor that the reader is motivated to read it themselves. After all, avid readers are always on the lookout for exceptional books.

A celebrity or famous individual may release a new book that interests a large number of individuals who rarely read at all. But, as a new author, you are much more likely to sell your book to the niche of readers who already read books in your particular genre. You'll need to identify the category that best suits your upcoming book, and you will need to select the proper genre(s) when you submit your book to online book retailers. To make the right choice, research book titles within the category you believe would be appropriate. Review their synopses and promotional materials.

As stated previously, when you are a newly published author, your initial copies will probably be sold to family and friends. But if you want to achieve substantial sales, most of your buyers must be complete strangers.

Remember: Your audience will be comprised primarily of three types of people:

- Avid readers. People who read at least one book every month. The books may be in paper or digital form.
- Casual readers. People who buy books when they are motivated to do so, primarily in paper form, about two to five books per year.
- Readers you reach through direct, one-on-one contact. You can reach them through speeches, seminars, conferences, presentations, special events, book expos and festivals, and book club meetings.

Understanding the nature of your reading audience will assist you in developing your future marketing and promotion plans.

CHAPTER 7

GETTING STARTED WITH YOUR BOOK PROJECT

Now that you are certain that you have a story to tell, how do you know you can actually write a book? How can you quickly and easily assess your writing skills?

Think of a book as a collection of dozens of paragraphs woven into an entertaining or informative story. Can you write three paragraphs on a single topic without struggling? Can you do so within one hour and in one sitting? If so, you probably can write a book -- or you can at least get started.

With that in mind, here are two important things to consider before you start your book project. First, be aware that the two hardest things about writing a book are: starting and finishing. There are millions of aspiring authors who start writing their books and never finish. Some get three-quarters of the way done and cannot muster the remaining words or plot scenes to wrap up their project. Some authors start three or four book projects and never complete them.

Second, be aware of a writer's greatest enemy: procrastination. Writers will often let days or weeks go by without writing any new words. The more time that elapses between writing sessions, the easier it is to end up with an only partially-written book. The best way to combat procrastination is to establish a consistent writing routine.

Some well-established authors who write full-time suggest writing a minimum of 1,000 words per day. However, for many aspiring authors, 1,000 words may seem daunting, and they may feel like they have failed if they don't reach this goal. The most important thing is that you work on your craft on a regular basis.

Establish a set time to work on your book each day. If you must skip a day, try not to skip more than one. Choose a quiet place and time to write. You might write only one paragraph or a few sentences per day. As long as your writing is consistent your chances of completing your book in a reasonable amount of time are good. The amount of time it will take you to complete your book depends on how much you write per session and the total number of pages or words you expect your book to ultimately include.

For example, if you anticipate that your book will have a length of about 200 pages, this is the equivalent of approximately 40,000 words. If you write 500 words per day and work on weekdays only, it will take you approximately sixteen weeks (or four months) to complete the draft of your manuscript. Once the draft is completed, you should then review your manuscript, reading it word-for-word and making your own edits. Get it as close to perfect as you believe it can be before you turn it over to a professional editor.

Be prepared for your editor to make significant editing recommendations. If you hire a professional, you should expect him or her to find every mistake that you have made. Once you receive the edits, incorporate them into your manuscript. Then give it one final, word-for-word reading before publishing. I always find a handful of mistakes at the very end of the process. It is much better to correct errors in advance of printing than to receive your galley (draft from the publisher) -- or worse, your published book -- only to find multiple typographical and grammatical errors.

Dallas author Brian W. Smith, who self-published several titles under the auspices of his own company, Hollygrove Publishing, before signing a book deal with Strebor Books, a Simon & Schuster imprint, gives aspiring authors this advice: "The only [concrete] advice a best-selling author can give you about writing a book is 'get a good editor.' Everything else (e.g., how to write a book, how long it takes, when to write, etc.) is simply that author's opinion. Find your own routine. Find your own writing spot. Write about the things *you* want to write about; I don't have to like [them]. Whether it takes 30 days or 30 months, work at *your* pace. Stop trying to follow someone else's blueprint; do what works for *you*."

Smith's advice is sound because every author's experience is unique. Some authors are able to complete a first draft within sixty days. Others need two years before they are done.

One self-motivating technique that keeps me from procrastinating is telling my friends and family that my book will be released on a specific date. I also inform my social media network of the release date through Facebook and Twitter posts. Once I have made the public pronouncement, I am obligated to abide by it because of my desire to maintain my reputation and integrity. I am obligated to complete the book and have it published close to that date.

Here is a simple technique to help you get started and envision your book: Think of your book as a human being.

- It begins with the **SOUL**, the concept for the book, its general idea and your main focus for writing.
- Next insert the **SKELETON**, the structure of the book. This is usually in the form of an outline. For non-fiction books, the outline consists of the chapter headings. For fiction books, the outline describes the plot and the major points of the storyline.
- Next is the **FLESH**, the muscles, cells, veins and arteries. These represent the internal workings where the structure of the book is filled in. If your book has fewer than 100 pages, it will appear to be a "booklet" and will need to be priced accordingly. Children's books are, of course, much shorter than standard books.

Finally, let's clear up some common misconceptions about book writing:

Misconception #1: You have to know exactly where your plot will take you when you get started.

Truth: The plot will often unfold during the writing process and changes to the plot will likely be made as the book is written. I often hear fiction writers remark that they don't know exactly what their characters will do until they complete their novels. Once you start writing, ideas will start flowing, and the plot will become clearer. If you get stumped during the process or suffer from what is known as "writer's block," then it sometimes helps to take a day off from writing. Take a walk, visit friends, go see a movie, spend an evening out to dinner with your spouse or significant other. These non-writing activities can often free your mind so that new ideas and concepts can flow forth.

Misconception #2: You have to be an expert in English.

Truth: Strong English skills are a good asset, but having a strong concept and plot for your book is more important. Content editors, copy editors and proofreaders are available to correct errors in plot organization, storyline consistency, grammar, spelling and syntax. However, if your English skills are weak, writing your book will be more difficult. If you have been away from writing for a while, you may want to take a refresher course at your local community college. There are also online webinars you can watch to brush up on your English skills.

To quickly test whether your word usage is accurate, a website known as Grammarly.com allows you to verify the accuracy of individual sentences and short phrases at no charge.

Misconception #3: You have to print thousands of copies of your book when you first publish it.

Truth: In this era of print-on-demand and eBooks, you can print a few dozen paper copies of your book initially and then reprint copies as needed. The profits you make from your book sales can be reinvested in printing more copies to sell. Some authors produce their books in eBook form only, but it is best to make your book available in both formats, even if your paper copy is only for display purposes.

Misconception #4: Your book will generate enough revenue to enable you to quit your day job.

Truth: While there are some authors who are able to make a living strictly by writing books, the vast majority of authors have day jobs that provide a stable income. Their book-writing activities are a passion or hobby and bring in additional revenue. Even authors who have published dozens of titles with major publishing companies will often maintain their full-time profession because of the stability, security and health benefits it provides.

Here are more tips for getting started with your book project:

- **Write about what you know.** Select a topic about which you are passionate and have an abundance of knowledge. Don't try to use vocabulary that is not representative of the way you would normally speak. And don't pretend to have expertise that you do not possess. Remember: Most books are written on an eighth-grade level.

- **Allow your words to paint the picture.** Develop your narrative creatively so the reader can visualize the characters and setting. Be descriptive. For example, here is a vague and uninteresting way of describing a male character in a book: "The man entered the room through the door." Instead, use adjectives and other descriptive words to paint the picture. "The tall, muscular gentleman confidently entered the door, wearing a three-piece, wool suit and carrying a black leather attaché case." In the latter example, the reader can actually visualize the character and identify with him.

- **When writing fiction, you decide how your story will unfold.** You determine the time period (past, present or future), the location (city and country, urban, rural, etc.), the setting (house, office, park, golf course, church, etc.), the characters, and everything in between. It is best to establish the basic general parameters for your book before you start writing because these parameters will determine the flow of your storyline. But feel free to make adjustments during the writing process. It's all up to you.

- **Set a goal for completing your book.** Establish milestones for the completion of substantial sections of it. For example, if your book has fifteen chapters, you might want to set a goal of one year for completion, with about four chapters completed each calendar quarter. Some authors utilize the "chapter-a-day" approach, setting a goal to complete at least one chapter during each writing session. The order and content of the chapters will likely change during the writing process, but this should not be cause for concern. *Nothing is engraved in stone until the book is submitted to the printer or publisher.*

- **Ask for feedback.** Once you have a few chapters written, ask two or three people whose opinions you respect to read your work and provide you with feedback. It is best not to ask family members or close friends because they will probably not be truthful for fear of hurting your feelings. Also, family and friends may not have the expertise to adequately evaluate your work. If your writing is not up to par or if your character development needs work, you'll want to know that before you spend several months working on your project.

Do not be offended if the comments are critical in nature. Constructive criticism is necessary to improve your book and get it as close to perfect as possible. It's best to get feedback from writing experts that you trust before proceeding too far down the road. Think of writing as a journey: It is better to change course after going a few blocks than to have to turn around after 100 miles.

- **A thesaurus is your friend.** Use a thesaurus liberally and consistently throughout the writing process to ensure variety in the terms you use in your narrative. A general rule is that one paragraph should not include the same descriptive term more than once.

- **Don't wait until your book is completely finished to get started on your cover design and editing.** In fact, getting your book cover designed early allows you to begin promoting your book *before* the publication date. This is the strategy adopted by major publishers. In advance of all release dates, publishing houses distribute catalogs highlighting the titles to be released in the next three to six months. The catalogs include the book's cover design, title and author, suggested retail price, ISBN, release date, and synopsis.

As a self-publisher, you can also utilize this strategy. That way, you can have readers awaiting your book's release and, in some cases, you can offer the book for pre-sale.

However, be cautious about pre-sales because you do not want to promise your book to readers on a specific date and not have it available on schedule. It would be best not to offer pre-sales until your book is completely finished and the editing process is underway. This will provide you with a more accurate estimate of the time frame for the book's release date.

Also, since the editing process may take at least a month or so, you may want to submit your manuscript to the editor you have selected when your book is about 80 percent complete. Then you will have approximately one month to complete the book and submit the final 20 percent to your editor. Utilizing this strategy can shave about two months off the publishing process.

- **Find ways to network with other authors.** There are writers groups across the country that meet on a regular basis. The odds are great that one exists in your geographic area. Craigslist.org, Meetup.com, and Linkedin.com are all useful tools for connecting with like-minded professionals. Facebook is a useful tool for locating people in your area with similar interests. Facebook also has a feature for locating groups of individuals that have already formed around similar topics. Local community colleges are good sources for writing and editing classes. Another option is that you could start a group yourself if one does not already exist within a close radius of your home or office.

Getting involved in one or more of these groups will not only give you motivation to get started, but it will also encourage you and sustain your motivation throughout the writing process. Some writers' groups actually critique members' work and provide feedback to improve the quality of each manuscript.

CHAPTER 8

COPYRIGHTS AND ISBNs

A copyright is the exclusive legal right, given to the original creator or to his or her assignee to print, publish, perform, film, or record literary or artistic works. A copyright does not protect facts, ideas, systems, or methods of operation, although it may protect the way these things are expressed.

As an author, it is best for you to obtain a copyright of your book to protect your rights and to secure your legal position in the event that another individual or author attempts to copy your work in the future. The worst experience in the world for an author is to spend years writing a book, only to have their work copied by someone else, either in part or in its entirety, without permission.

A copyright exists from the moment the work is created. You do not have to receive your copyright certificate before you publish your book, nor do you need permission from the Copyright Office to place a copyright notice on your book. However, if you wish to bring a lawsuit for infringement of a U.S. literary work, you will need to register your copyright with the U.S. government.

Although basic copyright protection is automatic, registration is recommended for a number of reasons.

First, many authors choose to register their works because they wish to have the facts of their copyright on public record and receive an official certificate of registration. Second, registered works may be eligible for statutory damages and attorney's fees in successful litigation. Finally, if you register your book within five years of its publication, it is considered *prima facie* evidence in a court of law, presumed to be true unless it is disproved.

In the interim, before you write the first line of your draft, create a title page for your book with your name as the author, "© Copyright," and the year you began writing to make it clear to individuals who obtain a copy of your manuscript prior to its publication that it is not available to be copied by others. NOTE: Titles cannot be copyrighted as there are many books and movies with the same title.

Your book does not have to be published to be protected and you can file your copyright with the federal government at the beginning of the writing process. To obtain the copyright for your book, visit the official website: www.copyright.gov. Copyrights can be obtained from the federal government with an electronic filing online for only $45.00. To register your book, submit a completed application form, a nonrefundable filing fee (which is $45 if you register online), and a nonreturnable copy or copies of the work to be registered. Since the copies of your book will not be returned, make sure you have other copies on hand, either in digital form or on paper.

You may also register your copyright in paper form via U.S. mail, but this process is more costly ($65) and takes twice as long to complete. The time the Copyright Office requires to process an application varies; however, average processing times are about three months for electronic filings and five months for applications submitted in paper form by U.S. mail.

For authors who write under a pseudonym or a pen name, there is no legal requirement that the author be identified by his or her real name on the application form. If you file under a fictitious name, check the box on the application that is marked "Pseudonymous" when giving information about the author(s).

Be aware that when you register your copyright with the U.S. Copyright Office, you are creating a public record. All the information you provide on your copyright application form is available to the public and will be available on the Internet.

The term of copyright for a specific book depends on several factors, including whether it has been published and, if so, its initial publication date. As a general rule, for books created after January 1, 1978, copyright protection lasts for the life of the author plus an additional 70 years.

How To Acquire an ISBN For Your Book

An ISBN is a unique identifying number that is assigned to every published book. It is used to simplify the distribution and purchase of books throughout the global supply chain. Each printed format for a book has a separate ISBN. This means that a book published in hardcover, trade paperback and mass-market paperback will have three separate ISBNs. If you publish your book through a traditional publisher or one of the many print-on-demand companies, they will usually provide you with an ISBN. Some will charge an additional fee for this service.

If you are self-publishing using a different method, you may obtain an ISBN through Bowker, the official source of all ISBNs in the U.S. Their website is www.bowker.com. The bar code that goes on the back cover of your book may also be purchased through Bowker. The bar code will be necessary if you plan to sell your book in brick-and-mortar stores.

ISBNs can be purchased individually (for single titles) or in blocks of ten (for publishers or authors who have multiple books). If you plan to publish more than one book, it is more cost-effective to purchase the block of ten ISBNs. ISBNs do not have an expiration date, so you can use them at any time. Any author publishing his or her book for commercial purposes should obtain an ISBN.

In the past, ISBNs had ten digits. Starting in January 2007, however, ISBNs were expanded to include thirteen digits. Currently, published books have both ten-digit and thirteen-digit ISBNs assigned to them, although the thirteen-digit versions are the ones that are used on books and incorporated within bar codes.

EBooks are not required to have ISBNs. The entities that generate the eBook (e.g., Amazon.com for a Kindle version), generate their own unique numbers for digital products.

CHAPTER 9

TEN CHARACTERISTICS OF A BEST-SELLING NOVEL

As an aspiring author, you need not reinvent the wheel to discover what characteristics are key to a best-selling novel. The following is a list of crucial elements of a successful book project. Most of these characteristics also apply to non-fiction books.

1. **A succinct, catchy title.** The title should provide a clue to the book's content; it should also pique the potential reader's interest and make him or her want to know more. In general, the title should be short, but long titles can also work if worded correctly. At the very least, your title should be memorable. You won't be able to benefit from word-of-mouth advertising if readers cannot remember the title of your book. It is also helpful if the title is unique, but it doesn't have to be. As mentioned in Chapter 8, only a book's contents, not its title, can be copyrighted. But you probably do not want to use the same title as that of a book that is considered a classic, in order to avoid confusion among readers.

2. **A professionally prepared cover.** Contrary to the old adage that "You shouldn't judge a book by its cover," readers do indeed do just that. The cover says one of two things about the book: Either 1) "I am a book that appears to be interesting. The author and publisher put some thought into preparing the cover so it would look like it was produced by a professional." or 2) "I am a book written by a first-time author -- an amateur -- who knows little about the publishing business and put this book together with little advanced planning. I may not be worth the investment and the potential buyer should proceed with caution." You don't want your book to be in the latter category. Covers that are too busy, too disjointed or not easily readable from a distance should be avoided. [Samples of good cover designs are included in Chapter 10.]

3. **Solid character development.** The reader should feel as though he or she knows the main characters in your story. The reader should be able to identify with and become emotional about the characters, and be invested enough in the storyline to continue reading until the very end. The information about the main character does not have to all be included in the first chapter of your book. Additional details can and should be woven into the story in subsequent chapters.

For non-fiction books, if you are the main character, readers should feel as though they know you very well after completing your book. Also, anecdotes – real-life examples of situations with real-life people -- are always helpful in non-fiction books. Pseudonyms can be used to protect the identities of individuals who would prefer to remain anonymous.

4. **A sound, well-developed plot.** What is your story about? The reader should understand this fairly early in the reading process. The story should flow in sequence, or at least, if the time frame goes from past to present and back again, it should be logical and easy to follow. The storyline should capture the reader's attention and make him or her want to continue turning pages.

5. **Chapter transitions.** One good way to keep the reader turning pages is with good chapter transitions. End each chapter with a tickler for what will happen next. To better understand chapter transitions, think of a soap opera or reality show series. At the end of each episode, there is an unresolved situation or a suspenseful scene that ends abruptly and requires you to watch the next installment to find out what happens. Writers should utilize a similar technique.

Through chapter transitions, you can keep the reader on the edge of his seat so he's reading your book into the wee hours of the morning. One of the most gratifying emails I received from a reader after finishing my novel, *The Genesis Files*, said this: "I started your book last night after dinner and now it's 4 am and I just finished reading *The Genesis Files*. Now I need to manage staying awake for Easter services. I really enjoyed the read and wait with [baited] breath for the next installment. Bravo!"

6. **Professional editing.** Every book needs to be edited. Even if you are a first-class writer with top-notch English skills, you will still need at least one additional pair of eyes to review your work. *Don't try to do this yourself and don't hire your child's elementary school English teacher as your editor.* Book editing is a specialized art form. Identify someone who has experience editing books, preferably within your book's genre. If you do not know someone personally, you can hire an experienced editor at an affordable cost by contracting a free-lance editor at www.upwork.com.

7. **Word-of-mouth buzz.** Once people start reading your book and enjoying it, they will tell others about it. This is the most effective and least expensive form of marketing. You can keep people talking about your book consistently by meeting with book clubs and groups of individuals that read your book and by effectively utilizing social media (Facebook and Twitter). Word-of-mouth advertising sells

a *lot* of books. More information about generating buzz by utilizing book clubs and social media is included in Chapters 18 and 19.

If you believe your book has solid content and is of good quality, ask online reviewers to review your book. When readers are browsing online book sites, they will often read reviews to see if a book is a worthwhile purchase. Potential buyers are less likely to purchase a book with an average review of three stars or less.

Most book reviewers provide this service free of charge if you send them a copy of your book. Be prepared that not everyone will like your book, but it's worth the risk, if you believe your book has merit. All of the major daily newspapers in the U.S. have book editors who manage this process. There are several book reviewers that you can locate on Amazon.com, or Facebook or via their own websites by conducting a Google search.

8. **Marketing, marketing, and more marketing**. Promoting your book is actually more important than the book's content. A book with average ratings and heavy promotion can sell millions of copies. (A recent example is *50 Shades of Grey*, which received only a 3-star rating on Amazon for the first installment of the series.) By the same token, an excellent book that is not promoted will sell few copies.

Some authors are under the misconception that simply listing their books on Amazon.com will result in sales. A listing on Amazon does *not* qualify as a marketing campaign. Since, as mentioned in Chapter 4, there are more than 20 million books listed on Amazon, expecting your book to stand out in that environment is the equivalent of expecting a needle to stand out in a haystack, or worse. The only way your book will sell on Amazon, or anywhere else, is if you have an ongoing marketing effort that will generate consumer demand.

There are a wide variety of marketing methods that self-published authors can utilize. These will be discussed in detail in Chapter 17.

9. **Availability/distribution**. Once your book is published, it needs to be available for people to purchase beyond the face-to-face sales you'll make. Distribution for your book guarantees that, once people are exposed to your marketing campaign and are convinced to purchase your book, they are able to obtain it through the industry supply chain.

In general, this is how the supply chain works. First, your book is published, either through a traditional publisher, a small press, or a print-on-demand firm. From there, it usually goes to a distributor. A distributor is a large company from which bookstores purchase their book inventory. Two of the largest distributors are Ingram and Baker & Taylor, although there are also other smaller distributors that either are regional or specialize in particular types of books.

Bookstores (or retailers like Wal-Mart and Target) also order directly from publishers, but distributors carry titles published by all of the major publishers, so ordering through the distributors simplifies the process for retailers. Bookstores include brick-and-mortar stores, like Barnes & Noble, Books-A-Million, and small independent stores, as well as online retailers, like Amazon.com. In the last step of the supply chain, bookstores and retailers make the books available for consumer purchases.

Without distribution, consumers will not be able to purchase your book, unless they do so directly from your website or from you at public appearances. Not having distribution will drastically reduce the number of books you are able to sell, since you cannot possibly meet all of your potential buyers face-to-face.

For the self-published author, availability on Amazon.com is essential. My experience has been that when my books were accepted and carried on Amazon.com, they automatically became available on the Barnes & Noble website (www.bn.com), even though I had never contacted Barnes & Noble directly. I have also never shipped any books to the Barnes & Noble web operation, even though the site indicates that sales have been realized, so I can only assume that Amazon provides shipping arrangements for at least some books listed on the Barnes & Noble site.

You might also try distribution through a few local, independent bookstores. There is a distributor that works exclusively with self-published authors and small publishing firms, Independent Publishers Group, that can expand your book's availability in brick-and-mortar stores. If you self-publish your book through CreateSpace (an Amazon.com affiliate), the site offers an expanded distribution option that includes availability of your book through Ingram, one of the largest book distributors in the world.

You might also contact websites that specialize in your particular genre to obtain information on their policies and procedures for inclusion among their online offerings. More information on convincing bookstores to carry your book is included in Chapter 20.

10. **Fresh material.** *Don't write a book you've already read.* Take a fresh approach, write a new story, and surprise your readers. Using a different angle or perspective will allow your writing to stand out from the pack.

Books within a particular genre tend to have similar structures or themes. For example, romance novels have simple storylines: Boy meets girl; they fall in love; they have some sort of conflict; they get back together; they live happily ever after. This storyline is predictable, but people who like romance novels enjoy the predictability. Yet, you can still manipulate the plot by approaching it from different angles. Perhaps the boy who meets the girl is disabled and is in love with a super model. Or, maybe the conflict that the couple experiences involves a natural disaster.

Whatever plot you ultimately create for your book, show the readers that you put some thought and time into developing your story. They will reward you by telling others about your work and by supporting your future literary projects.

CHAPTER 10

BOOK COVER DO's AND DON'Ts

Despite the old adage, potential readers *do* judge books by their covers. The cover separates the serious, experienced writer from the inexperienced, amateur writer. But you don't have to be a celebrity to produce a professional-looking product. To get an idea of how a professional cover should look, examine covers from authors who are writing full-time and are published by major publishing houses.

Your book sales will suffer if you fail to hire a graphic artist with experience specifically in book cover preparation. The following are mistakes you should avoid in your book cover design:

- Small print, not readable from a distance
- Script fonts, distorted fonts or fonts that are not easy to read
- Too much empty space
- Too busy, competing concepts and images
- Incorrect grammar in title or subtitle
- Small author photo (should be on back cover)
- Solid black background, no color contrast

EXAMPLES OF EYE-CATCHING COVERS

DO's

--Simple, clean graphics

--Clean imagery

--Bold colors

--Title and author's name clearly readable

--Subtle symbolism

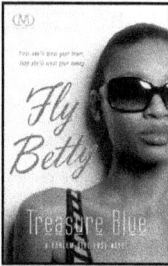

DO's

--Title and author's name are clearly readable

--Good color contrast

--Image makes a statement

--Model's skin is airbrushed

--Corporate logo in top left corner, inconspicuous

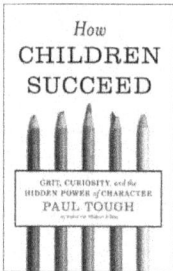

DO's

--Imagery is symbolic of title and subject matter

--Eye-catching and intriguing

Freelancers' rates for book cover designs start at about $200. If you have not developed a relationship with a professional graphic artist, Upwork.com (www.upwork.com) is a good source to identify graphic artists and editors for your project. There are hundreds of freelance professionals who will bid on your project and who can provide you with quality work.

Some graphic artists in foreign countries will offer very inexpensive pricing for book cover design. However, an American designer is going to be more familiar with the professional standards and nuances of the U.S. In addition, communicating with a native English-speaking contractor will make the process go much more smoothly.

Request that potential freelancers submit a digital portfolio of their work and look for artists with specific experience in creating book covers, including back cover and spine. Use caution and discretion when hiring a freelance contractor, regardless of his or her country of origin.

CHAPTER 11

THE MECHANICS OF DEVELOPING YOUR NOVEL

For a first-time author of a work of fiction, sometimes the most challenging aspect is determining exactly how to start the book. The first chapter of a book is vitally important as readers' attention spans today are shorter than they were in previous decades. In a novel, something usually must happen right away to hook the reader, so the first few pages are crucial. Here are several ways to start a novel and whet readers' appetites so they will want to continue turning pages. You may start with one of the following:

- A dramatic scene
- A prologue: Describe a scene that occurred in years past that has relevance to how the book will begin
- The main character self-reflects and describes his life or childhood
- A dialogue between two of the main characters

Once you develop your opening chapter, the following are some additional tips to help you develop your plot:

- Keep your plot and storyline simple and sequential. Complex storylines can ruin the reading experience. (Remember: The shortest distance between two points is a straight line.)
- The existence of too many characters combined with a lack of character development can *ruin* any work of fiction.
- High-quality, realistic and engaging dialogue is extremely important. Pay close attention to the details of interactions between characters.

Developing Your Characters and Storyline

In most works of fiction, there are two key roles for characters:

- **Protagonist:** The lead character who occupies most of the scenes in your book and whose life or escapades the book chronicles; the person with whom your audience will most likely identify; also known as the hero or heroine.
- **Antagonist:** The bad guy, the villain, the one who creates problems for the protagonist; one who represents or creates obstacles that the protagonist must overcome. May be an individual, a group of individuals or an institution.

There may be more than one protagonist and/or antagonist in a story. In some books, the villain is the main character, and that is okay.

The other characters in your book should complement the adventures of the protagonist and antagonist. For example, these could be a spouse, child, best friend, family member, co-worker, acquaintance, etc.

1. Write a couple of paragraphs describing the essence of your story. You should have a general idea about the beginning, middle and ending, although these can and likely will change as you actually write your story. The paragraphs are for the purpose of forcing you to think cohesively about the direction your story will take. These paragraphs may also serve as a draft of the synopsis of your book. (More information regarding developing your synopsis is detailed in Chapter 14.)

2. In developing your characters, imagine the type of person you want your protagonist to be. Be descriptive.

   - What does he look like? Where did she grow up? What about his background has a bearing on the situation you are creating in the story?
   - Who is the protagonist's significant other? Are children involved?
   - Who does the protagonist interact with regularly? A spouse? A co-worker? A friend? The antagonist?
   - Where does most of the action occur in your book? In the home? At work? At

church? At a night club? On the freeway? In the gym? At the park? The action can take place in a variety of locations as the character goes from place to place. After all, it is unlikely that the protagonist is homebound.

- Put your protagonist in a situation in which he has a lot at stake. This could be a lost job, a life or death situation, a health crisis, the betrayal of a friend, a cheating spouse, or an out-of-control child. Your readers should care about your protagonist; they should spend nail-biting, breath-holding moments reading your book and hope the main character triumphs.

- Create the scene and describe it in detail. Make sure the scenes you create match the storyline. For example, if it's summertime, don't have the characters wearing clothes that are made from wool or suede.

- You might create a biographical sketch for each character in your own notes, but don't include this information in the book for minor characters. The protagonist and antagonist are the ones that readers really need to get to know. Limit your lengthy character details to those two individuals or entities.

- Create several twists and turns in your storyline to keep the reader turning pages. An air of unpredictability is what makes for a great novel. The last thing you want to do is bore your readers.

- The next to the last thing you want to do is confuse your readers with a story that is disjointed. Don't meander or get sidetracked when developing your plot. Don't let your storyline get lost in the forest or in a maze. Keep the plot on the main road to reach the final destination (the story's climax or ending).

- Catchy phrases make a novel memorable. These phrases may come to mind at random times during the writing process. Write them down in your journal so you will not forget them.

CHAPTER 12

ESSENTIAL ELEMENTS IN A WORK OF NON-FICTION

If your book is a work of non-fiction, some of the same principles that apply to fiction are still applicable. However, there are some essential elements that are specific to non-fiction books.

1. Non-fiction books start with a premise or idea that is then supported by research and factual information.

2. Most non-fiction books should have a table of contents. The table of contents should mirror the outline you've created for your book, which should include the major elements in some sort of sequential order.

3. Non-fiction books are enhanced by quotations from experts in the relevant fields of study. Quotations should be original, if possible, based on telephone or in-person interviews or emailed questionnaires. Ask the individual's permission to be quoted. This can be done via e-mail, which will provide a paper trail in case there is a legal dispute in the future. This means that you should make a list of experts, contact them, interview them (phone interviews are

fine) and include quotations from those interviews within the body of the narrative.

4. Use reference material and include footnotes or endnotes. This lends your book more credibility. The book can be based on your opinion or observation, but it needs to be supported with factual information. Also, don't borrow ideas or facts from others without giving them credit via footnotes.

5. Your book should be as original as possible and stem from an original idea, concept, or angle about your topic. You should not duplicate ideas that are already available in abundance. Conduct research on already written books that are similar to the book you are writing to see what is already available on the market.

6. Start with an introduction that establishes the purpose of your book, your reasons for writing it, and what you hope readers will gain after they are done reading it. Your introductory paragraph should be powerful and draw the readers in. Tell them why you wrote the book, why the information you provide is vital and unique, and how it can enhance their lives or expand their reservoir of knowledge.

7. Keep a journal or a file to write down ideas as they come to you. You can also use the notes feature on your cell phone to quickly jot down thoughts so they will not vanish from your memory. Ideas for books often come to writers spontaneously as they are running errands, in

business meetings, shopping at the grocery store, attending seminars, at church, visiting friends or family, etc. Keeping a journal or other note-taking device handy will ensure that your ideas do not vanish into thin air, never to be recalled again.

CHAPTER 13

SELECTING A PRINTER OR PUBLISHER

Once your manuscript is complete, or perhaps even while you are still in the process of writing your book, you will need to select a publisher. Although you are self-publishing, you obviously will not be the one to print copies of your book. You will need a publisher for this purpose. Print-on-demand publishers allow you to publish professional-looking copies of your book in the most cost-effective manner, i.e., at a low price but also without requiring you to print hundreds of copies.

What is print-on-demand? This is a relatively new practice that was made possible by recent advances in technology. In years past, books were printed on full-size printing presses, some of which were so massive they required two people to operate them. Digital printing technology has since become high-quality and state-of-the-art. A slick, professional-looking paper-back or hardcover book can be printed in small quantities and at a low-enough cost that both the author and printing company are able to make a profit.

Some print-on-demand companies will allow an author to order a single copy of his or her book at the discounted wholesale price. Others may have a minimum print run of about 50 copies. In either case, the investment in printed copies of your book will be much lower than what you would spend with a traditional publishing company.

Here are some notes of caution regarding print-on-demand publishers. Be prepared to spend a substantial amount of time formatting your book so that it has a professional look. If you are not comfortable doing your own formatting, you may need to pay a professional to do it. These fees will need to be added to your budget.

In addition, some publishers will assert that authors' books will be available through Barnes & Noble and other brick-and-mortar stores. While this statement is technically accurate, placement does not occur automatically. The Barnes & Noble website will usually include the book in its online inventory; however, the book will only be available on bookshelves in the actual stores if there is a substantial demand among local customers. Otherwise, customers can call Barnes & Noble, order the book by phone, and wait approximately one week for the book to arrive at the store.

The following are names of several print-on-demand companies, along with their locations, websites, and general pricing and policies. Online tools and templates are available on all of these companies' websites that allow authors to upload their manuscripts, in either Microsoft Word or PDF format. Most provide formatting assistance for an additional fee. All these companies produce a high-quality product and have received above-average ratings by self-published authors who have used their services.

Print-on-Demand Publishers

Amazon KDP – An Amazon-affiliate, this entity offers a full array of author services, including book cover design, editing, and formatting assistance. Its online, do-it-yourself tools provide authors with a low-cost option for publishing. Once the manuscript is uploaded and formatted, a proof can be ordered and shipped to the author for a minimal cost. Once the proof is approved, the author can begin ordering printed copies in both paperback and hardcover (if the book is at least 75 pages).

The books are automatically available for purchase on Amazon.com, and the author receives a royalty on each one ordered. The author purchases books at a per-copy price of less than $5.00 each (for most paperbacks with fewer than 300 pages) and there is no minimum order requirement. KDP also offers the option of making the book immediately available in eBook form for Kindle ereaders at no additional cost.

Instantpublisher.com offers the standard print-on-demand programs offered by its competitors. A unique feature of InstantPublisher.com is its series of online video tutorials to assist the author in navigating the publishing process. The company also offers a variety of binding styles for its books, including spiral, saddle-stitching, and three-hole punching. The minimum order is 25 copies. The per-copy cost of printing a minimum order of a 200-page book is about $10.00 per copy. Pricing is considerably less per book for larger quantities.

iUniverse.com offers publishing packages ranging from $899 to $4,449. All packages include one-on-one author support, customized book covers, ISBN assignment, worldwide book distribution, and digital formatting (eBooks). However, the packages include the minimum quantity of printed books; additional copies cost extra. iUniverse also offers other services, such as editorial, marketing and publicity services, and custom video production. iUniverse sets the suggested retail price for your book based on the page count and pays a royalty of 10 to 20 percent on books sold through its site.

iUniverse.com merged with AuthorHouse.com in 2007. This company also offers authors expensive (from $2,000 to $15,000) advertising and marketing options. Book sales for new authors rarely justify these high costs, so proceed with extreme caution.

Lulu.com offers print-on-demand services as well as a wide range of publishing options, such as editing, book cover design and marketing services. The company also provides expanded distribution and eBook publishing, with distribution to the Apple iBookstore and Barnes & Nobles Nook. In addition, Lulu.com prints hardcover books, photo books and custom calendars. There is no minimum order requirement, but the price structure is much more attractive for quantities of at least 100 books.

Outskirtspress.com offers customized publishing packages for authors who prefer to work with a publishing expert throughout the entire process of creating their book. Their customized packages include book cover design, formatting, an ISBN and bar code, an author web page, expanded distribution and a few copies of the author's book. Once the book is published, authors order their copies at a discounted price. The company also offers premium services, such as ghostwriting, book tour management, marketing, and printing of promotional materials.

Traditional Publishers

If you are uncomfortable with the prospect of self-publishing, there are many small to medium-sized publishers who will accept your work. These companies are different from print-on-demand publishers because they actually manage the publishing process and print a pre-determined quantity of your book. Some charge a fee for their publishing services. Others pay a small advance and then pay royalties on book sales. The following publications provide extensive information regarding publishers to whom you may submit your manuscript.

1. *2022 Writer's Market* by Robert Lee Brewer - $30.00
2. *2022 Novel and Short Story Writer's Market* by Amy Jones - $30.00
3. *2022 Children's Writer's and Illustrator's Market* by Amy Jones - $30.00

4. *The Christian Writer's Market Guide 2022* by Steve Laube - $29.99

These books are updated annually and are available through most online and brick-and-mortar booksellers. They provide detailed information regarding publishers' areas of specialization, submission requirements, websites and website appropriate contact information.

CHAPTER 14

WRITING A FIRST-CLASS SYNOPSIS

Your book's synopsis is extremely important. The synopsis is the two- to three-paragraph description that will be included on the back cover and on websites that carry your book. Generally, it will be the marketing pitch that readers will use to make their purchase decisions. If your book's synopsis piques the readers' interest, they are more likely to make the purchase. If, on the other hand, your synopsis is poorly written or boring, readers who are contemplating the purchase of your book may quickly move on.

A good starting point for developing your book's synopsis is to read synopses written by major publishing houses for books within your same genre. After reading several of these, you will get an idea of the elements that should be included in your synopsis and the approach that is generally used. Your synopsis should be short and to the point.

A synopsis is *not* an excerpt. Do not take a few paragraphs from the beginning of your book and think your work is done. A synopsis is a summary of the general points of the book, but it doesn't reveal any secrets. It is a tool for selling, not storytelling. Your objective is to woo readers, motivating them to purchase your book.

One major mistake many authors make when developing a synopsis is making it too long. In these cases, the description of the book goes on and on, giving the potential readers so much information that they feel overwhelmed. The author's belief seems to be that the more the prospective reader knows about the book, the more likely he is to buy it. In actuality, the opposite is the case. Readers know how a professional synopsis should be presented. If yours veers too far outside the norm, it will be a red flag signaling that your book is written by an inexperienced author.

In a first-class synopsis, there is rarely a single word wasted. Continue to tweak your synopsis until you get it just right. Have a professional editor review it to make sure your wording and grammar are correct. One of the absolute worst things a new author can do is publish a book with a synopsis on the back that is riddled with misspellings, and incorrect English and syntax.

Once your synopsis is complete, you can start using it to market your book prior to its publication. Post it on your website and your Facebook and Twitter pages, and submit it to whatever online data file your publisher makes available for upcoming titles. Include a shortened version of the synopsis in print advertising, as well. Consistency in your marketing messages with a succinct synopsis will go a long way toward solidifying your branding efforts for your book and for you as an author.

CHAPTER 15

THE BUSINESS SIDE OF WRITING

As a self-published author, you must always think of your book as a business venture. You will spend hundreds (perhaps thousands) of dollars writing and publishing your book. You should expect a return on your investment.

As an author, you are self-employed, as opposed to being a full-time or even part-time employee of a publisher. This means you are subject to the same challenges all self-employed people face. You have no guarantee of either a steady income or work, no company-provided life insurance or health benefits, and no company stock options, bonuses, 401(k), profit-sharing plan, or pension plan. You have no paid vacation, sick days or maternity leave. (Of course, if you have a full-time job and perform your author duties part-time, then presumably you have benefits through your employer.)

In addition, you must assume all responsibility for providing the above benefits for yourself, as well as paying self-employment taxes, since you will not have an employer contributing to social security benefits based upon the fees you earn as a writer.

One of your first steps in establishing your business is creating a name for your venture and registering it with your county clerk. A sole proprietorship name, or DBA, should suffice initially. The cost to register your business and create a unique name should be minimal. In most states, the cost is less than $20.00.

With a legal business name, you can open a bank account in the business name and more easily deduct your business costs on your income tax return. The Internal Revenue Service requires that, in order to deduct home office costs, the area designated in your home must be used exclusively for business purposes. It doesn't have to be an entire room, but you do need to use the area exclusively for your business.

Keep track of your revenue and expenses from your book venture using an accounting software program or a ledger. Much of the activity related to your book projects will be deductible, such as the cost of printing books, travel expenses, gas and mileage, office supplies, and technology (e.g., cell phones, tablets, laptops, WiFi, Internet access) – even some of your clothing can be deductible if it is deemed essential for you to conduct business as an author. Extravagant clothing, such as Prada or Coach purses or Jimmy Choo stilettos, would not apply because they would not be deemed reasonable for the writing profession, unless you are already a millionaire and need those items to maintain your million-dollar image.

Since your book is essentially a business, giving your book away for free is a no-no, unless you are doing it temporarily as an incentive toward a larger goal.

Setting the Price for Your Book

Don't overprice or underprice your book. The standard price for a trade-sized paperback is about $15.00 if the page count is 150 page or more. For less than 150 pages, the going rate is about $12.00. A hardcover book sells for between $25 and $30. However, for a new author, a hardcover version may be a poor investment. Few readers are willing to pay $30 for a book written by an author they do not know.

The price ranges for eBooks are broad, from as low as $0.99 for a self-published eBook with a low page count, to as high as $12.99 for an eBook version of a newly released hardcover book by a major publisher. I recommend that you don't cheapen your work by charging $0.99 for your eBook. Price your book somewhere in the middle, between $4.99 and $7.99, depending on the page count. In general, the cost of your eBook should be about one-third the cost of the print version. In addition, newly released eBook titles should be priced higher than older titles (also known as "backlist" titles).

Maintaining Your Website

Although social media does fulfill many of the functions of an independent website, establishing a website using your author name and/or the name(s) of your book as the URL (or domain name) is still highly recommended. A website provides you with total control over the content of your message and the format in which the information is presented.

Keep in mind that establishing a website is like leasing real estate on the Internet. You purchase your domain name for either a one- or two-year period and it must be renewed before it expires. Otherwise, your website will no longer be accessible. A message saying, "No longer available," will be displayed, and the public will not know whether you are still publishing books. Many will assume that your books are no longer available. This lapse in service should be avoided. The cost of domain renewal is very affordable – less than $20.00 per year.

Develop a Marketing Budget

One of the most needed and most overlooked aspects of book publishing is marketing. Marketing is necessary to gain exposure among readers so they will have an opportunity to buy your book. Without marketing, readers will not know that your book exists.

There are many different forms of marketing and several are discussed in detail in Chapters 17, 18 and 19. However, what is most important is that you develop a marketing budget. Set aside a specific amount to spend on your marketing efforts each month. Your budget should be based on your disposable income once your essential household bills are paid. In other words, do not spend the money designated for your car payment on your marketing efforts.

Once you develop your marketing budget and plan and get started, it may take two to three months before you start seeing actual results. Do not expect to spend $100 and sell a thousand books overnight. Marketing does not work that way. Targeted, cumulative and repetitive marketing sells books over time. Before you expend resources on marketing programs, be sure that the companies you are considering have solid reputations and have been in business for a number of years. There are a lot of fly-by-night entities that claim to assist authors with marketing when, in reality they have no client base or expertise.

Realities Regarding Income Expectations

All authors have a dream that they will one day achieve the status of millionaire as a result of their book-writing activities. We tend to remember the legendary tales of the authors who wrote a couple of books and were offered a six-figure, multi-title book deal. The reality, however, is much more sobering.

According to a 2015 survey by *Guardian*, the average self-published author makes less than $1,000 per year. In fact, a third of them make less than $500 per year. [28]Average annual earnings were just $10,000 a year, and that amount has not changed significantly over the past five years. This amount, however, is substantially skewed by the top earners, with less than 10 percent of self-published authors earning about 75 percent of the reported total revenue and half of writers generating a personal income of less than $500. Fortunately, most authors do not write for the money; they write for the love of putting their ideas on paper and creating stories that others can enjoy. Yet, the survey revealed some interesting patterns among those authors whose incomes were well above average.[29]

- Romance authors earned 170 percent more than their peers.
- Authors who were female, educated and in their early 40s were the top earners.
- Those who were among the high earners were also prolific writers, churning out an average of 2,047 words a day, compared to 1,557 for the rest of the survey respondents.
- Self-published authors who received help (paid or unpaid) with story editing, copy editing and proofreading made 13 percent more than the average author. Help with cover design increased earnings by an additional 34 percent. In other words, making an investment in professional assistance for your book adds to your overall income as an author.
- Established authors who self-published only some of their titles earned 2.5 times more than authors who went straight to self-publishing. This is understandable because of the name-recognition factor.
- As stated above, 75 percent of total royalties generated from self-publishing went to about

10 percent of authors. This means that those who are good at self-publishing are very good, and those who are new to the book industry arena will likely get a slow start as far as revenue generation is concerned.[30]

A realistic assessment of your potential sales and income as a self-published author, relative to those of other writers in the industry, will alleviate frustration and disappointment as your pursue your part-time or full-time writing career.

CHAPTER 16

HIRING A GHOSTWRITER

If you have an idea for a book but don't believe you have the writing skills to actually produce one, you have the option of hiring a ghostwriter to write the book for you. In the ghostwriting arrangement, you retain all rights to the book and your name goes on the book as the author. The writer is hired to transform your ideas and concepts into a published product.

A ghostwriter can cost between $1,000 and $5,000 or more, depending upon the length of your book, the complexity of the subject matter and how much of their time will be required. There are a variety of methods a ghostwriter can use to create your book.

1. Utilize a draft manuscript that you have written, refine it and produce a finished product;
2. Develop an outline for the book, with your assistance, and then obtain information from you, enhancing it with research and supporting documentation; or
3. Conduct and record a series of interviews with you and other individuals pertinent to your book's content, transcribe the information and then develop it into a book.

If you are interested in hiring a ghostwriter, Upwork.com is a good place to locate a credentialed professional. Be sure to have your ghostwriter sign a standard non-disclosure agreement (NDA) before commencing work. You can obtain a template for an NDA online at www.lawdepot.com.

CHAPTER 17

EFFECTIVE MARKETING TECHNIQUES

As a newly published author or one who has garnered limited exposure, keep in mind that when you sell your book you are really selling *yourself* – your enthusiasm, your knowledge, your passion and your writing ability. You have not yet established a reputation in the book industry.

More importantly, no book sells itself, no matter how brilliant the writing. A book is just like any other product: It must be marketed to be sold. In that regard, there are a variety of cost-effective marketing methods you can utilize to promote your work.

1. **Email or eblasts**. Although consumers are bombarded with an inordinate amount of spam and unsolicited email, sending email or eblasts to targeted lists is still one of the most cost effective methods of advertising. The key is to send the communication to lists targeting a specific niche. This niche should be interested in reading books in general, and the types of books you specifically publish. You can develop your own list over time by collecting email addresses from individuals you meet in

person or online. You can also utilize fee-based services from credible companies that offer this option.

2. **Print advertising**. Like email, print advertising is most effective when in a publication that has a targeted audience suited to the subject matter of your book. Publications with large circulations (100,000 or more) have advertising rates that are generally beyond the reach of most self-published authors. Also, even if these funds were spent on advertisement that was large enough to be noticed, the return on investment would not come close to matching the funds expended. However, with print advertising you do get the added advantage of longevity and the ability of the end user to share the printed copy with others.

3. **Press releases**. Preparing a press release announcing the publication of your book and distributing it to relevant news organizations may land you one or more radio or print interviews. If you are fortunate, you could even land a feature story in a magazine or newspaper. Interviews and news stories add credibility to your book and can be included in your media kit or portfolio.

4. **Book trailers**. Like movie trailers, book trailers are videos that encapsulate the essence of your book's content. They can be good marketing tools if the production is professional and captivating. Be sure to hire a

video production company with experience preparing book trailers. Price ranges vary widely from a few hundred dollars to thousands of dollars, so you will have to shop around based on your budget.

5. **Facebook and Twitter promotions**. After you develop an audience via social media, Facebook and Twitter can serve as excellent tools to promote your work. These companies also have paid options to help you develop an audience, but proceed with caution. You can test a marketing message using Facebook's "Boost Post" option (only available for fan or business pages, not for personal pages) with a low-cost promotion of $10 to $20 first. If the test yields positive results, you may want to proceed with a more aggressive campaign.

   You will want to build your audience based on people who have an interest in your subject matter, so quality should be more important than quantity when you are building your base. More information regarding social media is detailed in Chapter 19.

6. **Snail mail promotions**. With the ever-increasing cost of postage, snail mail is no longer the most cost-effective option for marketing books. However, if a group of authors is able to collaborate on a mailing in which all of their books are featured, a snail-mail campaign could still be viable. The key to any successful snail-mail marketing campaign

is the mailing list. List brokers who specialize in consumer products have lists of book buyers among their offerings. You can investigate these sources online via a Google or Bing search.

7. **Business cards, bookmarks and postcards.** All authors should have at least one of these items designed and printed by a commercial printer, to be used as handouts for readers and business contacts. Vistaprint.com offers packages of 250 printed business cards, using online design templates, for as little as $20.00. Local printers can also provide these services, and you can contact them for price quotes and delivery times.

8. **Book expos and festivals.** Book events, such as expos and festivals, can be a good way to not only sell your books, but to also make valuable contacts in the book industry. Established events that have already built an audience and attract large numbers of attendees will usually reap the best results. It is important to be actively engaged with attendees and not simply sit behind your table. Zane says it best: "At book fairs, you can't sit there like a prima donna and expect people to buy your book." Also, be sure to factor all event costs (e.g., table registration, event tickets, airfare, hotel, ground transportation, and book printing) into your budget for planning purposes.

9. **Speaking engagements**. Speaking engagements are another way to reach a target audience. Whether you are a featured speaker or one of a few authors on a panel, the audience attending the event is likely to purchase your book if they enjoy your presentation and would like to hear more about your ideas and published books.

   Develop a Power Point presentation about you and your book. Contact some organizations in your area about speaking at one of their upcoming meetings, stipulating that you'd like the opportunity to sell your books at the end of the meeting. Organizations are always looking for guest speakers and this is a good way to sell multiple copies of your book in one sitting.

CHAPTER 18

MARKETING TO BOOK CLUBS

Book clubs, also known as reading groups, are small, informal groups of readers who meet periodically to discuss a book they have read. The clubs may range in size from as few as five members, to as many as one hundred members or more. Some book clubs are part of larger entities that have chapters in a number of major cities. But most are organized by one or two individuals who invite their book-loving friends to join them in their reading enjoyment. Most have female members exclusively, but some are co-ed.

Book clubs are an excellent way to create word-of-mouth buzz about your book because they are self-selecting groups of avid readers. They also represent a viable marketing option because they provide authors with the opportunity to sell multiple copies of their books at one time.

From my experience marketing to book clubs as a publicist for other authors, as well as for myself in regard to my own novel, I have found that many clubs' members are reading books in digital form using e-readers, rather than in paper form. In some instances, the entire club read my book in digital form. For a well-known author, the club members will often want autographed copies and will purchase a paper version for that reason.

Here are some helpful tips on how to get book clubs to select your book for their group.

- Develop your own list of book clubs, which could be local or elsewhere. You should be able to locate a few book club lists online or via Facebook.
- Focus on local book clubs first. Book clubs in your area should be enthusiastic about supporting local authors. If you are able to get local clubs to read your book, you will be able to meet with them face-to-face and receive valuable feedback.
- For out-of-town clubs, offer the option of a telephone conference call between you and the members. This can easily be done via cell phone, or you may utilize a free service for the conference call. Freeconferencecall.com is a free service that allows up to 96 participants at one time. The only cost to the club members would be the minutes expended on their cell phone plans.
- Contact the clubs via e-mail or Facebook private message and introduce your book to the facilitator. Request that they consider your book for a future club selection.
- If you know someone in a book club, ask her or him about the selection process. Different clubs have different procedures for making a

selection. For some of them, an individual member is responsible for selecting the book of the month and each member is assigned a different month. For others, club members vote on the books they will read. For still others, the group selects the books for the entire upcoming year and announces the list in January or on a designated anniversary date.

- Be aggressive, persistent and determined, but also respectful and patient. The selection process takes time and you will not usually get immediate results. Follow up with the book club several times until you receive a response. The response could be "yes," "no," or "contact us later." If the club indicates that your book may be considered in the future, be sure to make a notation on your calendar, and contact the club in a month or two to see if a decision has been made.

- If you have the opportunity to meet with a book club, be sure to take pictures and post them on your Facebook and Twitter accounts. These photos help with branding and marketing and will help solidify your position as an established author.

- After the meeting or conference call, be sure to send the club's facilitator a formal note of thanks via email or snail mail. Do not send a text message, as this is a much more informal means of communication.

- You might consider purchasing a book club list or an e-blast service from a credible source. Cushcity.com, one of the largest websites focusing on African-American books, has an internal list of 1,200 African-American book clubs. The company provides an e-blast service and also allows authors to purchase a subset of its master list (about 200 book clubs) in Excel format for personal use only. The list is not available to publishers, marketers, or publicists.

Marketing to book clubs will help you expand your reading audience and multiply your book sales. In addition, it is an extremely enjoyable and gratifying experience to meet with people who have invested in your work, enjoyed what you have written and express interest in reading more of your work.

CHAPTER 19

THE IMPORTANCE OF SOCIAL MEDIA

Social media, primarily Facebook and Twitter, is the best method to reach large numbers of people in a cost effective manner. Becoming a social media expert is both an art and a science. Social media marketing doesn't have to be daunting or intimidating. It's quite simple to get started and can actually be lots of fun, if approached correctly.

Do not let social media frighten or intimidate you. Despite some of the horror stories you may have heard about social media, for the most part, you do not have to observe or participate in any activity that you find objectionable. To the contrary, social media allows you to connect with like-minded individuals, on a worldwide basis, essentially for free.

Here are seven tips for getting started with social media marketing:

1. **Become familiar with the major vehicles for social media.** According to the World Economic Forum, the most commonly used social media tools are Facebook, Twitter, LinkedIn and blogs, in that order. Facebook is the most massive social media networking site,

with a growing population of more than 1.8 billion monthly active users.[31]

Twitter is known for short communications (a maximum of 140 characters) to a network of followers about current events or personal activities. LinkedIn, which boasts more than 600 million monthly active users, is used primarily for communication among professionals and is not designed for business-to-consumer marketing. Blogs are online vehicles for disseminating information on a regular basis. Blogs allow for more lengthy communications than do the other vehicles.

2. **Consult with someone who has social media expertise.** If you're really serious about social media marketing, seeking the advice of someone who has experience in the field will save you a lot of time. Hearing about the benefits of social media is one thing; becoming proficient in this medium is quite another. There are a number of experts in the field, including marketing guru Pam Perry, whose hands-on approach to bringing novices up to speed in the social media arena is among the best. A brief tutorial of about two to three hours can save you weeks or months of frustration and misdirection.

3. **Develop a marketing communications strategy.** Social media can be used for all sorts of communication that can attract potential customers. You can use it to advertise special

sales and promotions, to tout recent benchmarks or publishing successes, to inform the public about news publicity you've recently received, or to quote a 5-star book review you received. Write down a plan for the first sixty days regarding your social media posts.

4. **Hit the ground running.** Once you've completed your social media marketing training, get started right away with setting up your social media operation. Don't procrastinate.

   Set up your Facebook page, or, if you already have one, enhance it with images. Complete your profile and info pages. In order to ensure that you have ideas for posts readily available, you can keep a Word file on your computer where you can store ideas for creative posts as they come to your mind. That way, you'll have some stockpiled for future use.

5. **Set up your Twitter accounts.** Tweets are designed for brief communication and are limited to 140 characters. You can set up Facebook and/or Twitter accounts so that you can post on one and the comment will automatically be posted on the other. This saves time and also ensures continuity among your messages. This link on the Sleeplessmedia website provides instructions on how to sync your Facebook and Twitter accounts.

6. **Create your blog and post your initial entry.** Don't feel as though you have to write a

thousand-word post initially. Many people make that mistake. They post one or two lengthy blog entries, and then they abandon the blog altogether because they feel like they've said it all or because it's simply too time-consuming to write that many words on a regular basis. Thousands of people have made this mistake, as evidenced by the abandoned blogs you'll find all over the Internet. Instead, make your entries relatively short -- about 250 to 300 words. That will leave you with more to say later.

7. **Inform friends, clients and associates**. To build up your Facebook fan base and Twitter followers, you'll need to inform your friends, clients and associates about your pages. This can be easily accomplished on both Facebook and Twitter via tools that are accessible on their websites.

Authors should do more via social media than simply promote themselves and their books, as this tends to be a major turnoff for potential supporters. Instead, authors should engage their audience in conversation regarding a variety of topics. Current news items, new films, family and relationships, accolades for friends – these are all topics that work well via social media.

Zane is critical of authors who use social media only for self-promotion: "All they [authors] do is go online and promote their books. They don't say anything about themselves and don't engage in conversations online." Don't let this be you.

There are three types of people who regularly utilize social media:

1) **Posters or commentators**. Individuals who post threads (conversations on particular topics) and photos on their Facebook timelines, or send messages via Twitter (also known as "tweets"). On Facebook, these threads will appear on the "newsfeed" of the friends of the original poster.

2) **Responders or commenters**. Individuals who respond to threads with comments, participating in the discussion or debate. Posters also tend to be responders.

3) **Browsers or observers**. Individuals who read the newsfeed and the comments, but do not post responses themselves. This represents the largest group within the social media population.

As an author, you should be a poster/commentator, since this will help you build your reading audience. People within your social media universe will get a sense of who you are, what you do, and how you think. In order to be effective as a social media participant, as an author you should post content that meets the following standards:

- **Readable and grammatically correct.** Remember: You're an author. If you are constantly posting information that is misspelled, is factually incorrect or contains multiple grammatical errors, it may affect your audience's opinion of your skills as a writer.

- **Targeted to your reading audience and supporters/fans.** Get to know your audience and their interests and hobbies. This is especially important as you build your network of friends. "Friending" (or sending a friend request) individuals with whom you have interests or friends in common is one of the major pillars of building your social media network.

- **Timely/relevant.** Stay abreast of current events and trends. Express your opinion about things that are happening *now*. Start a discussion and a dialogue. Strategically mention your book projects and activities, but do not constantly talk about yourself. Give your Facebook friends and Twitter followers information that can benefit *them*. Be willing to share. In other words, be "social."

- **Consistent.** Post to social media at least three to four times per week -- daily is best. People who frequent Facebook start following the posts of the commentators. You want people to log in and look for your recent morsels of wisdom, interesting stories, or humorous tales.

- **Shareable.** Post items that people will want to share with others. A picture is worth a thousand words -- images and videos are good because they are eye-catching. The more your posts are shared, the bigger your social media network will become.

- **Visual.** Post photos of yourself and what you're doing, places you've gone, people you've met, and activities that are relevant to your profession. Use captions or comments to describe what took place.
- **Appropriate and in good taste.** Do not post nude photos, profanity or vulgarity on social media that you will later regret. (Note: This rule applies whether or not you are an author!)

Once you garner a substantial number of fans/friends (a minimum of 500), you can also utilize Facebook for other purposes. For example, you can utilize it as an online focus group to test ideas and concepts. A lot of people on Facebook are willing to offer opinions, are knowledgeable on a variety of subjects, and would love to participate in something that does not require a lot of time.

Have a graphic artist design a Facebook cover for your page. The "cover" is the graphic at the very top of your Facebook page. It can include an image of your book, or any other type of advertising message you desire. It's an inexpensive way to brand yourself and promote your work.

Social media marketing is becoming an increasingly important force in our culture. Implementing the above seven tips will get you onto the playing field instead of sitting on the sidelines. Once you get your social media effort off the ground, you'll need to maintain these efforts for both the short term and the long term. The following are some additional things to keep in mind as you maintain your social media marketing:

Be proactive. By placing the properly linked Facebook, Twitter and blog logos on your website's home page, you will make it more convenient for your existing and potential readers to receive your marketing communications. This will increase your reach and add to your client base.

Be synergized. To increase efficiency and ensure that your marketing message has a multiplying effect, all aspects of your social media campaign should work in synergy with one another. The lengthiest message should be the foundation for the other outlets that allow for only brief communication.

For example, if you are promoting an upcoming author signing, you could produce a short video and post it on YouTube. Your blog post could provide detailed information about the event -- its purpose, the main speakers, and the date, time and location. Within your blog post, you should include links to your YouTube video, website, relevant resources and contact information.

Then, on Facebook, you could post a more concise statement about the event, providing a link to either the blog or the YouTube video that can go out via the news feed to your Facebook friends. The beauty of marketing with social media is that once your message propagates throughout the Internet, which usually takes about 24 hours, it can be accessed via Internet searches.

Social media networks are here to stay, and their influence will definitely increase as more individuals use these resources to stay connected to family, friends, business associates and clients. Be sure that you are leveraging social media and positioning yourself and your book projects for success.

CHAPTER 20

APPROACHING BOOKSTORES ABOUT CARRYING YOUR BOOK

As mentioned in Chapter 2, the odds of getting your book on the shelves of major bookstores and retail chains across the country are slim to none for self-published authors. But there are opportunities to get independent bookstores to carry your book. However, you will need to have a clear understanding of how independent bookstores operate and what they look for in books they consider adding to their retail inventory.

First, bookstores, just like other enterprises, are in business to make a profit. They only make a profit if they sell books. They are not like libraries; they are not funded by the government, and they do not collect books to keep them on their shelves. Books have to turn over, or be sold, for the bookstore to benefit. You probably believe your book is one of the best ever written, as most self-published and first-time authors do. But, all of that enthusiasm won't amount to a hill of beans if no one wants to buy your book.

Also, keep in mind that bookstores are constantly receiving calls and packages from other self-published authors who are trying to get exposure for their books. With the recent explosion in the number of self-published authors, the competition is fierce. Therefore, it is important that you develop creative ways to make your book stand out from the pack.

Second, every bookstore owner wants to carry books that are popular and in demand. If customers come into their stores and cannot find the books they want, they will go elsewhere or purchase them online. A bookstore cannot afford to have shelves filled with books that no one wants to buy or has not heard about. Therefore, it is important that you demonstrate to a bookstore owner that there is demand for your book.

The demand can be demonstrated in a variety of ways. Some self-published authors have had friends and others contact bookstores to inquire about the availability of their books. Having friends actually go into the store to make inquiries about your book is even more effective. Based on this demand, the bookstore owner may then contact a distributor to order a few copies of your book. That is why having your book available through a major distributor is so important. A bookstore owner is not likely to take the time to contact an individual author to inquire about a book and purchase it directly from him or her.

Once the book is available at the bookstore, however, the owner still has to see some sales results. Otherwise, the unsold copies will be returned to the distributor for credit toward the purchase of future inventory.

Third, be sure to conduct research in advance about the bookstore you are approaching. Make sure the bookstore carries books like yours. For example, if a store carries only used books (Half Price Books, for example), it is not one that you should contact. Or, if a book carries only children's books, and yours is adult fiction, do not waste your time and theirs by asking them to consider your title.

It is best to start your efforts with bookstores in your area because the owners may be more willing to include the works of local authors in their inventory. This will also provide you the opportunity to meet the store owner face-to-face. However, it is best to arrange an appointment with the owner rather than drop by the store unannounced. Most independent bookstores have small staffs and the owners are generally busy throughout the day.

If you contact the store via email, be sure to personalize your communication. Do not address the recipient as "Dear Sir and/or Madam." In fact, it is best to call first, find out the name of the owner or manager, and address him or her directly in the email. Although you may be able to find that information listed online, there is a good chance that personnel at the store may have changed, so it is better to double check.

If you do send a mass email to a number of stores simultaneously, be sure to use the bcc feature on your email (rather than cc). The bcc option means that the individuals who receive the email will know neither the identities of other recipients nor the number of individuals who are on your list.

When you contact the bookstore, let the owner know what types of marketing you are doing for your book. For example, if you have a recent or upcoming interview scheduled on a local radio or television station, let the owner know. If any local newspapers have published articles about your work or you have speaking engagements scheduled, let them know that as well.

Prepare a package that you can submit to bookstores for consideration. Your package should include:

- A standard twin-pocket portfolio that can be purchased from any office supply store
- A new copy of your book in saleable condition
- Copies of newspaper, magazine or blog posts about you and your book
- A one-page document that includes your photo, brief biography, list of accomplishments, places where your book is currently sold, any best-seller designations or awards, etc.
- A business card or postcard with your contact information

Since there is a cost involved in preparing your package, send it only to the most promising prospects. It is best not to send out "blind" packages, meaning that you have not spoken to the store owners so they are not expecting to receive them. There is no need to waste valuable resources on lost causes. Do not allow your enthusiasm to override your business acumen.

Offering the book on consignment initially will be more attractive to the business owner than requesting that they purchase a quantity of your book at a wholesale price because it minimizes the owner's risk. Proceed with caution. The factors to consider when making a consignment arrangement are discussed in detail in Chapter 2. Offer to start with a small quantity of between two to five books to minimize your own risk as well. If the initial books sell within a reasonable amount of time, then you can request that future orders be paid for either upon delivery or within thirty days.

After sending or leaving your package with the bookstore, be patient. Wait a couple of weeks before following up. Do not call the owner every day asking if he or she had an opportunity to review your package. It will do more harm than good.

Consider hosting a book event at the store and inviting your friends and associates to attend, if the store owner will allow it. Bringing in new customers will be noticed and appreciated and will increase the chances that your book will be added to the inventory.

Finally, accept the fact that not everyone will like your book and not every store will carry it. If the bookstore politely declines, be gracious. If they do carry your book, please do not call the store every day asking if any copies have sold. Do not go into the store and rearrange copies of your book on shelves to make it more prominent. And definitely do not go into the store, hang around and try to badger customers into buying it. However, if you believe sales of your book could increase if grouped with other books of similar subject matter, you might suggest this to the owner. As professional booksellers, though, they have probably already considered this.

The following are a few stores from each region in the U.S. that will allow self-published authors to submit their books to the stores for consignment arrangements. Also included is information regarding each store's consignment policy.

Carmichael's Bookstore (Louisville, KY) – Louisville's oldest independent bookstore. Store owner Carol Besse says they will accept almost any book on consignment. "We'll put it on the shelf. We usually start out with 10 copies."[32]

The Dock BookShop (Fort Worth, TX) – Specialty: African-American literature. Store co-owner Donya Braddock says that they couple their consignments with promotions because "we find that, without promotion, the book just sits there." The store has a promotions department, and promotional options include marketing through their radio show, and via social media, and eblasts. The author starts by submitting books and once those sell, the store does its disbursements and buys wholesale directly from the author. The consignment arrangement allows for one full year for the five copies to sell.

Literary Joint Bookstores in Maryland (3 locations): The first step is for an author to send a nonreturnable copy of the book to the submissions address included on the store's website. Included with the book should be contact information, publisher information, the wholesale price and the printing method. After a 60-day review period, authors can follow-up with the store representative, but it is preferred that no contact be made before that.

Lyon Books (Chico, CA): The consignment policy is to accept books for any authors within 60 miles of the store. Consignment checks are disbursed every two months.[33]

Nubian Bookstore (Atlanta, GA) – Located in Southlake Mall, this bookstore specializes in African-American literature. The owner, Marcus Williams, accepts books by self-published authors on consignment. Three to five copies are required for consignment; based on sales, the store owner decides if a reorder is warranted. Authors do not have to be Atlanta-based and the store does allow authors to schedule book signings.

Tattered Cover Book Store (Denver, CO) – Their consignment program is focused on local authors and small publishers in the Denver area. The book must first be reviewed by a staff representative. Once it is approved, a $30 administrative fee is charged for the consignment and the first consignment term lasts for 90 days. At the end of the first term, the sales of the title are reviewed to determine future placement in the Tattered Cover's ordering process. The book may be renewed on consignment or returned, depending on its sales.

Watermark Books and Café (Wichita, KS) – Store owner Sarah Bagby says, "No questions asked, we'll take five copies of a book on consignment." The store keeps the books on the shelves for 90 days. "If they sell, we'll get back to the author right away and reorder. If they don't, the author needs to pick up his or her books."

The Written Word (Colorado Springs, CO) – The store requests five copies minimum and does not limit itself to Colorado. "We will take books from anyone, and if someone with a book out would like to use our venue while traveling to this area, they only need to ask."[34]

CHAPTER 21

OBTAINING A BOOK DEAL WITH A MAJOR PUBLISHER

After authors successfully self-publish one or more titles, many of them are interested in parlaying that success into a book deal with a major publisher. This is a viable option as publishers tend to be risk-averse and prefer to invest in authors who have a track record of generating sales and building a reading audience. Proven sales in the range of 5,000 to 10,000 copies are good threshold numbers for approaching a major publisher.

Most major publishers require that you hire an agent and submit a book proposal. A book proposal is normally the table of contents (for non-fiction books), the chapter outline and the first three chapters of the book. However, for first-time authors (you would be considered a first-time author if you have not published through a major publisher, even if you have multiple self-published titles), publishers and agents require that the entire manuscript be submitted, which means your book must be completed.

A publisher will often opt to re-release the title that you have self-published as your first project, which means that you already have a completed manuscript. For the re-release, the publisher would edit your book according to its specifications, design a new cover and develop a distribution and marketing strategy. If you are able to obtain a book deal based on one or more of your self-published titles, the publisher will generally sign you to a multi-book deal of at least two books – your self-published title and one additional book to be determined. In general, they will expect these books to be released within one year of each other.

First-time novelists should be aware of the many steps that are involved in the book publishing process prior to the book's release: editing, copy editing, typesetting, proofreading, cover design, endorsements, catalog inclusion, listing with Books in Print, press release distribution, advance review copies to book reviewers and others in the industry, etc. Once you have signed a contract with a publisher, it will generally take 12 to 18 months for your book to be released.

As stated previously in this book, with the rapid changes in the publishing industry, book deals are not nearly as attractive and numerous as they once were. Unless you are already among the top 5 percent of authors who have proven they can sell books and have a built-in audience, the amount you will receive as an advance is going to be relatively small – about $5,000 or less. But you will have the resources and connections of a major publishing entity at your disposal, and this does give you an advantage.

Acquiring An Agent

Literary agents tend to be hidden in plain sight in the book industry. Everybody hears about agents through news reports of authors who obtained book deals, but obtaining access to one yourself can be challenging. In general, they work on a referral basis and it helps if you can be referred to one or more by a respected member of the book industry. Many well-established agents will not accept unsolicited manuscripts from authors.

Your relationship with your agent will be similar to a business partnership or marriage in that the agent receives a percentage of every dollar you make, for every book of yours for which he or she is able to obtain a signed publishing contract, for the entire life of the book. This means that the agent receives a percentage of your advance and all of your royalties. The standard rate that agents receive is 15 percent.

A reputable agent should never require you to pay upfront fees for them to represent you and your manuscript, and should never refer you to an editor who charges you for his or her assistance. Professional agents will represent you if they believe your manuscript has a high potential of being accepted by a publishing house, since this is the only way the agent gets paid. The agent is gambling on the chance that your manuscript will be accepted and will sell.

However, it is strongly suggested that you hire a lawyer to review the agent's contract before signing it. Not all agents are honorable and an unsuspecting author can easily get burned. And because of the symbiotic relationship authors have with their agents, even an established author can be duped.

For example, the Pulitzer Prize-winning author of *To Kill A Mockingbird*, Harper Lee, sued her literary agent in May 2013, claiming he tricked her into assigning the copyright on her book to him.[35] The lawsuit was filed in federal court in Manhattan against Samuel Pinkus, the son-in-law of Lee's long-time agent, Eugene Winick, who had been Lee's agent for more than 40 years. When Winick became ill in 2002, Pinkus diverted several of Winick's clients to his own company.

According to the lawsuit, in 2007 Pinkus "engaged in a scheme to dupe" the then 80-year-old Lee into assigning her *To Kill A Mockingbird* copyright without any payment. Pinkus engineered the transfer of Lee's rights to secure himself irrevocable interest in the income derived from her book and to avoid paying legal obligations he owed to his father-in-law's company for royalties that Pinkus allegedly misappropriated. To date, the book has sold 30 million copies, but, in recent years, Pinkus has not provided royalty statements to explain money earned by the book.[36]

Do not assume that every agent will operate with integrity. Request references and contact them. As an author signing with a literary agent or an attorney, you should diligently adhere to the old adage: "Let the buyer beware."

The following are some methods authors can utilize to identify a literary agent:

- To obtain a comprehensive listing of literary agents, consult the following book, which is available at the library and through most online and brick-and-mortar booksellers: *2018 Guide to Literary Agents* by Cris Freese, $29.99.
- If you have a personal relationship with a published author or belong to a writers group, ask the author to recommend an agent.
- Review magazines geared toward the literary industry, such as *Publishers Weekly, Book Business* and *The Bookseller*, for profiles or listings of agents.
- Submit entries to writing competitions that offer consultations with agents as part of their award packages.
- Visit websites that provide online directories of literary agents, such as <u>Agent Query</u> and the <u>Association of Authors' Representatives</u>.
- Attend writers' conferences and literary conferences that include seminars or panels where agents are presenters. Some conferences offer writers an opportunity for one-on-one sessions with agents.

One Self-Published Author's Experience

To better understand how the publishing industry works, it is always helpful to learn from the experiences of others. In that regard, best-selling author Curtis Bunn's publishing saga is instructive.

Bunn's first novel, brokered through an agent, was titled *Baggage Check*. The book was published in 2001 by A&B Books, a small publishing house that specialized in distribution of books with African-American themes. (The company has since ceased its publishing operations.) *Baggage Check* was number one on *Essence* magazine's bestseller list in August 2001. Earlier that year, Zane, a then up-and-coming author who would later head Strebor Books, wrote a glowing review about *Baggage Check* on Amazon.com, stating, "Curtis Bunn has penned an excellent novel on relationships from a male's perspective."

A decade later, after self-publishing another novel titled *That Was Then, This Is Now*, Bunn recalled that complimentary review and contacted Zane about an idea he had for another book, *A Cold Piece of Work*. "I sent her and her sister, Charmaine Roberts, [Strebor's] editorial director, a few chapters and other pieces to a proposal," said Bunn. "A few weeks later, I received an email from Zane with an offer."

A Cold Piece of Work was released in July 2011, followed by *Homecoming Weekend* in September 2012. In April 2013, Bunn submitted a proposal to Strebor for a book he had started writing called, *The Old Man in the Club*. "After about three weeks, I received an offer with a surprising caveat—they wanted to offer me a two-book deal."

Bunn's experience demonstrates that the environment for acquiring book deals remains fertile -- that major publishers are still looking for talented writers with interesting stories to tell. He found his foray into self-publishing helpful in terms of learning all aspects of the book industry, and has some cogent advice for aspiring authors.

"First, do not be discouraged. Remember that this is a business charged by subjective thinking." But, adds Bunn, "Provide a polished, edited manuscript that is well-written, thought-provoking and [that] tells a unique story. Manuscripts that have those elements have a much better chance at attracting the attention of agents and editors."

CHAPTER 22

FUTURE TRENDS IN BOOK PUBLISHING

The digital age has ushered in new opportunities for self-published authors. Authors have more control over their destinies and options will continue to increase.

In the coming decade, eBooks will become the format of choice for millions more readers. Those under age 35 have begun to rely heavily on their smartphones, tablets and other digital devices for most of their communication and entertainment. This includes reading books, listening to music and watching movies.

A significant shift has occurred in the eBook landscape in that is the decline in the usage of dedicated e-readers. Americans increasingly turn to multipurpose devices such as smartphones and tablets when they engage with eBook content. Also, smartphones are playing an especially prominent role in the e-reading habits among minority groups and those who have not attended college.[37]

Two additional developments are harbingers for the future. First, major publishers have begun offering titles in eBook form only and will compete with Amazon and other digital book providers to offer more frequent royalty payments. HarperCollins' William Morrow division will launch Witness, a digital-first imprint for mysteries and thrillers, in October 2013. Witness is part of HarperCollins' "Impulse" line of books, which also includes digital-first romance, sci-fi/fantasy and young adult books. The company also said that as of August 1, it will pay all of its digital-first authors royalties on a monthly basis, competing with Amazon Publishing.

The second development comes from Bowker. A few months ago, the company announced its "Book As An App" program, which allows authors to offer their books as smartphone apps, thereby creating another source of revenue. After set-up, Bowker handles the rest, including having your book manuscript transformed into a downloadable app and submitted to the iTunes app store. Once your app is in the store, you earn 50 percent royalty from all sales.

Additional opportunities will certainly abound as the methods by which consumers receive data become more personalized and accessible. As you embark upon your writing career, stay abreast of current and future technological trends. Be sure you are informed about developments within the book industry that may impact your publishing options. If you continue to improve your craft, you will receive your share of good fortune, and contribute to the body of literature for years to come.

ABOUT THE AUTHOR

Gwen Richardson has been an entrepreneur and book industry professional for more than 15 years as an author, editor, publicist, marketer, retailer and event planner. She has worked with self-published and best-selling authors alike to help them develop their books' themes, organize the content of their books, and develop their marketing strategies.

Gwen has been twice-nominated for NAACP Image Awards for Outstanding Literary Work. She has a B.S. degree in marketing from Georgetown University and is based in Houston, Texas.

Visit her website: www.gwenrichardson.com

Communication via email is welcome. Email the author at gwenrichardson123@gmail.com.

ENDNOTES

[1] Rebecca Brandeywyne, "Advances and Royalties: How Authors Are Paid," www.brandewyne.com

[2] Brandeywyne

[3] "Quick Guide to Book Contract Trouble Spots," www.publishlawyer.com

[4] "Quick Guide to Book Contract Trouble Spots"

[5] Jeremy Greenfield, "When Self-Published EBooks Become Best-Sellers," Dec. 3, 2012, www.forbes.com

[6] Greenfield, 2012

[7] Alison Flood, "Self-Published EBook Author Becomes Amazon's Top Seller," Feb. 8, 2012, www.guardian.co.uk

[8] Jeremy Greenfield, "Self-Published Title Hits No. 1 on EBook Best-Seller List for First Time," March 10, 2013, www.digitalbookworld.com

[9] Sammy S., "J. K. Rowling Net Worth," June 1, 2012, www.therichest.org.

[10] Wendy Coakley-Thompson, "Author Millenia Black Predicts A Positive Paradigm Shift Out of the Ashes of Seg-Book-Gation," Dec. 31, 2010, www.examiner.com

[11] Coakley-Thompson, 2010

[12] "Millenia Black's Suit Against Penguin Has Been Resolved To 'Her Satisfaction'. . ." May 13, 2008, www.karenknowsbest.com.

[13] Tim Sanders, "The Surprising Truth About How Publishers Buy Books," Nov. 27, 2012, www.netminds.com

[14] "Book Publisher Goes To Court to Recoup Hefty Advances From Prominent Writers," Sept. 25, 2012, www.thesmokinggun.com

[15] "Book Publisher Goes To Court to Recoup Hefty Advances From Prominent Writers

[16] "Random House Sues P. Diddy Over Advance," 2005, www.billboard.com

[17] Brady Dale, "Despite What You Heard, the E-Book Market Never Stopped Growing," January 18, 2017, Observer, www.observer.com, Accessed Oct. 12, 2017.

[18] Ivana Kottasova, "Real books are back. E-book sales plunge nearly 20%," April 27, 2017, CNN, www.money.cnn.com,

Accessed Oct. 8, 2017.
[19] Ferris Jabr, "The Reading Brain in the Digital Age: The Science of Paper Versus Screens," April 11, 2013, *Scientific American*, www.scientificamerican.com.
[20] "Book Stats Highlights 2012," Association of American Publishers, www.publishers.org
[21] "Book Stats Highlights 2012
[22] Valerie Peterson, "Self-Publishing Your Book: Reasons to Self-Publish Your Book," 2013, www.publishing.about.com.
[23] Brady Dale, 2017.
[24] Brady Dale, 2017.
[25] Eric Weiner, "Why Women Read More Than Men," Sept. 5, 2007, www.npr.org
[26] Brady Dale, 2017.
[27] Laura Miller, "Books Aren't Dead Yet," March 20, 2013. www.salon.com
[28] David O., "Why Most Self-Published Authors Make Less Than $1,000 Per Year," January 28, 2020, *Entrepreneurs Handbook*, www.entrepreneurshandbook.co, Accessed Dec. 27, 2021.
[29] Alison Flood, "Stop the Press: Half of Self-Published Authors Earn Less Than $500," May 24, 2012, www.guardian.co.uk
[30] Flood, 2012
[31] Rosamond Hutt, "The world's most popular social networks, mapped," March 20, 2017, World Economic Forum, www.weforum.org, Accessed October 8, 2017.
[32] Jason Boog, "How To Sell Your Self-Published Book in Bookstores," April 20, 2012, www.mediabistro.com
[33] Boog, 2012
[34] Boog, 2012
[35] Erin Geiger Smith, "To Kill A Mockingbird Author Lee Sues Her Agent Over Copyright," May 3, 2013, www.mobilebeta.reuters.com
[36] Smith, 2013
[37] Andrew Perrin, "Book Reading 2016," September 1, 2016, Pew Research Center, www.pewinternet.org. Accessed October 12, 2017.